GAUDÍ
THE MAN AND HIS WORK

First English Language Edition
ISBN 0-8212-2627-4
Library of Congress Catalog Card Number 99-72457

Bulfinch Press is an imprint and trademark of Little, Brown and Company (Inc.)

PRINTED IN SPAIN

GAUDÍ
THE MAN AND HIS WORK

Text by
JOAN BERGÓS

Photographs by
MARC LLIMARGAS

Preface by
JORDI RIBERA I BERGÓS

Introduction by
MARIA ANTONIETTA CRIPPA

A Bulfinch Press Book
Little, Brown and Company
Boston • New York • London

INDEX

BERGÓS ON GAUDÍ

THE AUTHOR OF
GAUDÍ, THE MAN AND HIS WORK

Jordi Ribera i Bergós

Gaudí, the Man and his work is something more than an analysis of the egregious Gaudí from the artistic point of view: the amusing anecdote, his childhood years, and the banal, everyday events; all in all, the human side of any great individual which can sum up their nature, some small obsession, any habit repeated over and over, or even a degree of defiance or transgressions unknown to the general public.

The chain begins with Gaudí the man; following on from here is the disciple and enthusiastic admirer of all to do with the genius, and this is where Joan Bergós comes into the picture, Bergós analysing Gaudí's life and work. Bergós, in acknowledged homage, attempting to ensure continuity for what time is already wrenching from our hands; wishing, perhaps, to resume what has been interrupted, to guarantee that the artist remains alive in our memory; and to validate all that is worth stressing in a wide-ranging book which does its utmost to leave nothing out of the great architect's biography.

Moreover, this new edition of *Gaudí, the Man and his Work* represents a particularly important link in the process of remembering Joan Bergós, on this occasion as an Art Historian specialising in the work of Gaudí. This process of recognition began in 1994, the centenary of Bergós' birth, when two monographic exhibitions were held in his home town of Lleida in his honour. The first, held in the *Paeria* or City Hall, was devoted mainly to Bergós' drawings and watercolours, with many original works and photographs being lent by his daughters Magdalena and Mireia. The second, installed in the Association of Architects' Sala Gosé, was dedicated to Bergós the architect and town-planner (his plans for new suburbs in Lleida and Seu d'Urgell are of particular interest; the latter city's came into existence in 1926). Then again, in 1995, the Cultural Heritage Office of the Catalan government published a short monograph on the architect, written by the present writer. This was by way of an attempt at finishing the fine work done by Carles Cardó in his monograph which, however, only dealt with the period up to 1928.

Moreover, this brief portrait of Joan Bergós must include a reference to his aesthetic position, which ranged from Gaudí's premises to those of *noucentisme*. The purity of Gaudí's influence was already visible in the first major jobs he did as an architect, in Lleida. Along with other young architects of the time, Bergós was drawn to Gaudí. In fact, as Bergós was to explain at a later date, "a number of young architects from the classes of 1915 to 1918, instructed by Gaudí in order to be able to continue his work on the Sagrada Família church, resisted joining the new trends then in vogue, producing works which followed Gaudí in features and mood. Lluís Bonet Garí, in the vaults and skylights of the *Bank* at no. 9, Passeig de Gràcia; in the chapel of the Garí property in Argentona, and in the plans for a monument to Prat de la Riba in Castelltreçol, which never came to be built owing to the critics' violent reaction against Gaudí; the author of these lines, in the wrecked *Sacramental altar* of Sant Llorenç parish church (1919); in the house of the *Baron of Alpicat* at no. 2, Rambla de Catalunya (1921), both in Lleida, and in the *St. Antoni Chapel* at Serc in Urgellet. Bonaventura Conill and Folguera i Grassi were closer to Gaudí in their simplification and synthesis than in their forms, carrying out interesting studies of Gaudí's aesthetic and philosophical ideals. And even in the early 60's, Bergós (along with another architect, E. Rosich) paid posthumous homage to Gaudí in the new tower of the old chapel of *Our Lady of Puig* in Sant Celoni (Barcelona): a slim pisciform tower topped by a star-shaped pinnacle with mosaic embossments. Between the limits marked by these two dates, Bergós had the opportunity to associate fully with *noucentisme*, under the influence of Galí and his Art School. On the one hand, he became imbued with the Classical spirit during journeys to Italy (1922 and 1933) and around the Mediterranean (1934), virtually obligatory in *noucentisme*. And while the conditions of the tender for the altar-baldachin project and presbytery refurbishment of the Seu Nova in Lleida (1924-25, destroyed in 1936, with a large input by Galí and the sculptor Rafael Solanich) specified that they were to be in the neo-Roman style, for the church, parish house and schools of Our Lady of the Port in Barcelona (1936, not finished until 1947) he voluntarily chose an airy cupola in the style of Brunelleschi, although unlike other architects such as Rubió i Tudurí, Pelai Martínez and Raimon Duran i Reynals, he was not a close follower of the great Florentine architect.

Bergós' close relationship with the city of his birth went beyond his work as an architect, to take in that of art historian. With great acumen, Josep M. Ainaud stated that "Bergós was very quick to realise the value and symbolism of that unique monument, the Seu Vella in Lleida, overlooking the Segrià from the top of the old knoll of Ilerda, profaned by the troops of Philip V, who used it as a barracks for his occupying forces. Gradually falling into disrepair, this old medieval monument was crying out to be restored, and it was individuals such as Bergós the architect, with his excellent works *La Catedral Vella de Lleida* (1928) and *L'Escultura a la Seu Vella de Lleida* (1933) who encouraged the army to leave the old cathedral and to begin its restoration".

However, it would be wrong to fall into the error of thinking that Francesc A. Galí and Gaudí were Bergós' only influences. As a matter of fact, Bergós also came under the influence of engineer, physicist and mathematician Esteve Terrades (1883-1950). First, when the latter set up the Institute of Applied Electricity and Mechanics (under the Catalan Regional Government), he invited our architect to teach the subject of Industrial Architecture. Later – when Primo de Rivera's dictatorship had closed the Institute – Bergós worked under Terrades while the latter built an underground line across Barcelona, and Catalonia's network of secondary railways. Joan Bergós admired the wide-ranging knowledge (his "polymorphous erudition" in his own words) of Terrades – whose privileged mind was unreservedly admired even by Einstein – as he did not limit himself to pure science and abstract thought, which he understood only as an exercise in conjecture. He also took an interest in applied science, confirmed by experiment. And even this applied science had then to be rounded off with a knowledge of literature, philosophy, music and the plastic arts (which of course is where architecture came in; he was most knowledgeable on the subject, to the extent that Bergós considered that he was "in reality" an architect).

One last individual who influenced Joan Bergós, less famous that the above but just as solid, was Josep Martínez Vallespí (1882-1964), a soldier, biologist and doctor from Lleida with ideas on re-educating the young physically and mentally; the architect met him through his father – Joan Bergós i Dejuan, travelling salesman, cultural promoter and poet - who became his best moral guide, sometimes acting almost as one of those private tutors that the great personalities of the Classical world had – a world which Vallespí was well-acquainted with (and despite having been a soldier, he was one of the first to opine that the Seu Vella should be restored).

While reading these lines, you will have seen that Joan Bergós' had a great many abilities. It has to be admitted that he was not equally proficient at all of them. For instance, his oil paintings are not brilliant, lacking light, while his watercolours are fine, and his drawings excellent, as will be seen from the ink drawings that he did especially for this book. He was also a keen music-lover and enjoyed reading, if we are to go by his library, which was not limited to professional works. It should be remembered that when his sight became too poor to read, some of us grandchildren or one of his daughters read for him.

And here we have him again, Bergós, enthusiastic disciple of Gaudí from his earliest days as an architect, but one also imbued with *noucentisme*; Bergós, with his wide-ranging knowledge, the unequivocal art historian, worthy architect and town-planner, accompanies us on what is always a fascinating itinerary through Gaudí who, thanks in some way to all, becomes a little less enigmatic with each day that passes.

GAUDÍ, BETWEEN CONTEMPORARY HISTORIOGRAPHY AND THE ACTIVE SEARCH FOR BEAUTY

Maria Antonietta Crippa

"Antonio Gaudí's greatness as an architect is to be found in his prolific invention of forms. The variety and expressiveness of these forms, taken as sculpture, would in themselves be sufficient to qualify him as an outstanding modern artist. But in fact, they were the result of unusual structural contrivances, the imaginative use of materials and a unified sense of decoration — three traditional attributes of the architect. If we then add to this his ability to use architecture to achieve such incorporeal effects as space, colour and light, we can see why the world of architecture has now turned its attention to his relatively sparse and almost forgotten works."[1]

In the dense forest of interpretations of the great Catalan's works, I find this succinct but exact definition formulated in the 1960s by the American George Collins, a fervent Gaudí scholar, a basic key to understanding the originality and historical authenticity of a "unique and unpredictable" genius, but one who is "not totally inexplicable".

In the conclusion to his essay, Collins writes: "Much more so than in the case of many other architects, his work must be experienced directly. Works such as Güell Park or the Colonia Güell chapel can be admired in the same way as paintings by an old master: after long visits and unhurried contemplation, the spectator is pleasantly surprised with the discovery of interplay in structure and surfaces. But, in general, is it possible in architecture to achieve these constant surprises and this continuous delight under the conditions that contemporary technology has imposed on builders? This is the question posed by engineers, architects and artists searching, each in their own way, for an answer here in Barcelona."[2]

For the leading lights of modernity, known until then as pioneers, the 1960s were a critical time, recorded immediately by historiography in the revision of the phenomenological conformations that took shape during the brief period between the two World Wars, or immediately after World War II.

It was at that time that Gaudí suddenly became known internationally, the centre of attention of working architects and critics, who saw in him a bearer of previously unsuspected or ideologically censured possibilities for expression.

Interest in him has continued to grow, extending far beyond the closed circle of architects and critics, far beyond the European horizon. It is no exaggeration to say that his architectural accomplishments have entered the common heritage, becoming enshrined in the collective range of imagery, kindling enthusiasm, perplexity and even conversions in artistic opinions. In other words, his images have become bearers of meaning.

Collins —along with many others— has become a spokesman for a widely shared reading that postulates the need for an extensive familiarity with the Catalan architect's works, that emphasises as self-evident his status as a genius on the basis of the unique and unpredictable qualities of his creations, that points out, albeit briefly, the relation between autonomous factors and heteronomous elements in architecture that makes it into a part of the ensemble of peoples' conscious expressions, that stresses the message of Gaudí's work —in the inextricable context of form, structure and decoration— in contrast with contemporary rationalist reduction.

The American scholar's balanced directness has its counterpart in the volume by Bergós published here, a counterpart that is just as valid in terms of quality and measure, but more complete in its direct testimony. The text, based on first-hand knowledge, combines an attentive reading of the Catalan architect's works with insights into his character and temperament, and observations on his cultural environment and life.

The author, a long-time friend of Gaudí, expresses in terms that retain their freshness the emotion and wonder of one who knew and admired this man, who was unassuming and introverted in his personal life, but openly communicative when it came to expressing the development of his imagination over the years, a man of exuberant brilliance with an exceptional visual culture and critical autonomy.

In revealing the moving intensity of the encounter between these two individuals, the book not only stimulates an appreciation of architectural creations, described in fine detail and with technical precision, but also the understanding of a certain cultural and religious vision.

Undoubtedly, the main witnesses here to Gaudí's greatness are, in the first place, his creations, but also in the foreground are his human qualities and temperament, which concentrate, as a crucible collecting and fusing the magma of imagination, unexpected architectonic figures under the control of full-fledged ability and talent that can be described, at very least, as rare.

The contemporary historiography of architecture is not overly familiar with such a reading. It is more inclined to a type of interpretation that leaves the artist's personality in the dark, to focus on the definition of overall historical lines that are considered valid as continuity or a break between tradition and innovation. At the most, it will analyse individual poetics, figurative systems with self-contained formal perfection that refer only in passing to the man himself and his experience of life.

Bergós's text has unquestionable worth and is reminiscent of the anecdotic pleasures of Giorgio Vasari's artists' lives, which are far from ingenuous, and the comprehensive vision interweaving Brunelleschi's temperament and inventive genius in the biography by his contemporary Antonio di Tuccio Manetti.

This sort of account is perhaps the most straightforward and effective manner of regaining a synthetic concept of what we call genius, in other words, the contribution of one individual that transforms the horizons of expressive potential for all.

As the Catalan writer Antoni Marì has pointed out, the apparent non-currency of the recovery of such a concept could serve an important function: "Today, the figure of the genius is held to be dubious and its idealism is considered to be excessive; today, since genius is not humanity's ideal, but since, at the same time, there is nothing to take its place, today, I repeat, is the best time to analyse the nature and characteristics ... (of) ... this human archetype, which was believed to transcend the human condition through sheer knowledge."[3] But in order for such a recovery to be effective, the interpretation must strike a balance between the various interpretive factors, must not veer into excessive lyricism, and must adhere strictly to the concrete reality of fact; this is, fortunately, the case in Bergós's text.

Although they use different methods, Collins and Bergós pursue the same end, seeking to redeem, undiminished, the strength of Gaudí's constructive and imaginative capacity, with even a view to a renewal of architecture.

Both of them venture beyond what Collins, in a very fitting definition of 20th-century architectonic modernity, calls "changing ideals", into the realm of existence consecrated without reservation to a stable concept of life.

The widely varying interpretations of Gaudí's works in contemporary architectural criticism are common knowledge, and would merit a much closer examination than may be undertaken here.

At first, they were admired only by his fellow-countrymen and ignored in international circles of criticism, with the exhibition dedicated to him in Paris in 1910 failing to make any significant impression. His originality, seen as surrealist or baroque, was soon noted in a few marginal articles.

The first authoritative works on the history of architecture in the 20th century, by Platz, Pevsner, Behrendt, and Giedion, which tended, up until the end of the 1960s, to focus on the precursors of an aesthetic modernity in harmony with the continuity of technological progress, long ignored Gaudí's works.

Beginning in the 1950s, at the hands of Bruno Zevi, who linked Gaudí's works to art nouveau and expressionism, they were gradually reintegrated into the history of the 20th century, a history that has since been subjected to continuous revision and has become more and more complex and less and less monolithic, arriving at the most recent analyses. On the subject of Gaudí's creations, writers have referred, among other expressions, to "disturbing prophecies", "pop architecture", or *ante litteram* abstract art, to the configuration of a "technique of the image" turned aside from the science of perspective derived from the Renaissance "to then base it on fantasy", to a "puzzling case of modern architecture", or to religious ideology taken to the extremes of sanctimony.

Since then, no architect or historian of contemporary architecture, regardless of whether they are attracted to Gaudí's work or repulsed by it, has been able to avoid its fascination.

We should not forget that it was Le Corbusier —as we are reminded by Giedion— who first opened his contemporaries' eyes to Gaudí's genius.

No less significant, and even more precise, is the appraisal made by José Luis Sert, a disciple of Le Corbusier and successor to Gropius in teaching at Harvard, in the U.S.: "We cannot go on building our cities solely of edifices that look like boxes and are inspired exclusively by the system of beams and pilasters. The continuing evolution of modern architecture will probably lead to an ever greater appreciation and importance of Gaudí's later experiments. Then his greatness as a pioneer and a precursor will be recognised."[4]

More recently, during the 1970s and 80s, his work has been re-evaluated even more openly and energetically, particularly in those historiographical circles that are capable of responding quickly to changing times. There remains an active but hobbled front of detractors who, nevertheless, cannot ignore him.

In this era, Ragon takes an exceptionally free approach, defending Gaudí's total modernity and, at the same time, rehabilitating other figures and styles, such as Charles Garnier and art nouveau.

His tracing of the roots of modernity to an 18th-century illuminism, open to the co-existence of symbolic and functional factors, was much in advance of more recent and now widely held opinions along these same lines.

He is also generous in his praise of turn-of-the-century artistic and architectonic creations, seeing in this period a blend of tradition and avant-garde that had previously gone totally unnoticed, pointing out, for example, the "abstract" character not only of pure geometry, as in Kandinsky, but also of Gaudí's work, such as in the ridge-trees and balconies of the Casa Milá.

Lastly, he gives an enthusiastic description of Gaudí as "a profligate megalomaniac, like Frank Lloyd Wright", "an architect, landscape gardener, sculptor, ceramist and collage artist, all in one", the proponent of a naturalism "taken to absurd extremes" in his conception of a "cathedral meant also as the embodiment of a synthesis of all styles and arts" and in his embarking on a direction in figuration that was totally at odds with his times, giving back "to the ancient column its tree-shape", in keeping with an concept that is, nevertheless, in itself "artificial, since his tree is counterfeit, a tree of stone and cement".

He sees Gaudí as an artist who was thoroughly imbued with the culture of his time, particularly with the same love shown in such different ways by Viollet-le-Duc and Ruskin for medieval architecture and with the current enthusiasm for "a fabulous Orient, the Orient of Gustave Moreau and Flaubert, the Orient of Salome", in a sort of architecture where "everything is decoration, everything is sculpture, everything is plastic poetry, even that which remains unseen".

The Sagrada Familia church "is, in spite of everything, a thoroughly extraordinary work. In his desire to modernise the Gothic style, Gaudí, who was a devout Catholic, succeeded in building one of the few modern cathedrals that are visible acts of faith. His brilliantly bad taste is given free rein in this building ... Philip II, who was so taken by Hiëronymus Bosch, would have loved Gaudí ... No other architect, with the possible exception of Ledoux in the 18th century, has ever taken animal and vegetable symbolism to such extremes ... Climbing the spiral staircases in the two towers (of the Sagrada Familia) is an extraordinary adventure. Because Gaudí thought of everything: as you climb, you are presented with a genuine show, a show with deliberate surprises, with astonishing vantage points ... Gaudí's vigorous faith was tinged with a pantheism that converts the whole of his work into an offering to God of the fruits of the earth."

Lastly, Ragon points out that Gaudí's life was uneventful in the extreme, "like Cézanne's, in that, in both cases, they were individuals whose intense internal life overwhelms the urgency and grandeur of their work".[5]

An exuberant imagination, a constructive and inventive genius, an ability to attain, freely and completely, the figurations of history, a fusion of rationality and symbolism, a communicative force strong enough to transform the architecture of a church into the testimony of an act of faith: these are the co-ordinates of an interpretation that remains open.

They are also the most obvious specific attributes of Gaudí's popularity, a popularity that is borne out by the impressive number of exhibitions dedicated to him, time after time, around the world.

In spite of this, there remains much to be discovered about Gaudí's work, with much ground still to be covered in the analysis of his choices, his imagery, and the constructive dimension that he put into practice.

In this regard, we must make at least one final point. Today, it is widely held that the realm of Catholic thought from the time of the Counter-Reformation, or Catholic Reformation, of the 16th and 17th centuries, until recently, was exceptionally harsh, giving expression to an ecclesiastical theology "so rigid and compact as to seem amour-plated and impenetrable ... a theology ... invested with a conceptual capacity totally removed from any possible stimulus for the poetic inspiration or artistic imagination".[6]

Fortunately, there is now an active theology that is "open, non-conceptualist, sensitive to the complexity and richness of symbolic and hermeneutic thought, a theology that is clearly richer in images than in ideas ... far from being closed in the staunch defence of a manner of thinking diametrically opposed to contemporary thought ...". Nevertheless, at least so far, "the stimulus meant to imprint the features of spiritual beauty on corporeal matter seems hesitant and indecisive". While there has been a reactivation in all contexts of a religious consciousness that has also stimulated the world of art, few styles have yet appeared that are capable of propagating exemplary spiritual creations. Gaudí anticipated in a prolific manner the current and as yet undefined circumstances, in spite of the fact that he found himself in an environment of Catholic theological thought that —and it must said— was not particularly helpful to him.

In the light of these considerations, his work appears as a miraculous revelation of "beauty converted into form", in the words of Hans Urs von Balthasar, the leading figure in 20th century theology.

The Swiss theologian has given us a prior and lofty-sounding definition of beauty, as an *incipit* to his theology, that can show us new values in Gaudí's architecture. Beauty, he says, is "the last word that the thinking intellect dares to pronounce, because it does no more than crown, as an infinitely resplendent halo, the double star of truth and good and their indissoluble oneness"; this is the "disinterested beauty" "in which we no longer dare believe", a beauty "that, at very least, demands the very courage and decisiveness of truth and good themselves".[7]

In our long-lived contemporary era, art has seldom attempted to give form to this beauty and thus fully revive the classical sense of form as the internal unity of natural and artistic phenomena.

It has seldom looked to nature and attempted to comprehend its organisational principle on any scale, much less paid any attention to the human form-figure, which is creation, as a sign of the divine, as a play of its revelation-concealment, recovering the traditional wisdom of European craftsmen.

Beauty —as a sign of transcendence, as an intimation of the glory of a hereafter, whose figure is hinted at in the splendour of nature and of art— has not been the focal point of art for the last two centuries, and even less so in the case of architecture, which has striven generously to build new cities —cities that are more hygienic, more rationally organised— for mankind.

I believe that this is the key to Gaudí's commitment, which returned a liturgical value to the creation of art, a value similar to the cosmic liturgy present in the imagery of the Catholic liturgy. He integrated into his expressive language the most disparate historical-artistic forms, recovered as syntagmata of a new visual language, in the pursuit of a universal harmony.

Along the way, his architecture, with its rigorous structure in terms of rationality and functionality, took on a playful quality, at times relevant and balanced, at times redundant.

When he assumed the responsibility of expressing his faith in a specific religious creed through architecture, without suppressing or lessening the importance of any technical or disciplinary aspect of his profession, Gaudí issued a far-reaching challenge, one that is still with us today.

He searched freely through the repertoire of contemporary images at his disposal; he generated new images through evolutionary exclusion of those already in existence; he gave exuberant shape to an intuitively sensed and liturgically experienced beauty, although one that was not adequately defined by a Catholic *Weltanschauung*.

His love of Greek architecture, of the Mediterranean essence, and his attempt, which can only seem to us an extravagant one, at merging Greek architecture with Gothic architecture, with the comparison between Orestes and Hamlet as its basic paradigm, are more comprehensible in the light of these considerations.

This was sensed by one of his contemporary, Pujols, who examined, although in a reading that tends somewhat too heavily towards esoterism and is, in my opinion, alien to Gaudí, the meaning of the Orestes-Hamlet parallel that was such a favourite of the Catalan architect.[8]

Orestes, the prototype of the human strength of acceptance of one's destiny, is the solar figure in which doubt fills the instant, like an imprisoned lightning bolt that is immediately absorbed by sudden decision, turning the will directly towards its goal.

In this capacity to give religious and aesthetic expression to the brilliance of vital energy, Orestes personifies the Greek temple, designed around powerful columns and a light without shadows, never captured by an interior space, outlining its external profile.

In contrast, Hamlet is the personification of the Gothic cathedral, with its interior space filled with the light of day and the shadows of night. His doubt does not emerge from the encounter with the complexities of reality, about which he must take decisions, but rather from his inner self, from his spirit.

From this perspective, Gothic architecture, the crowning achievement of the Middle Ages, is seen as a deformation of the classical style, seeking an intensification of vital energy in the conquest of inner space. The Gothic experiment remains incomplete in northern medieval culture, incapable of the solar determination of the Mediterranean. In the search for an aesthetic unity of the interior and the exterior in architecture, a unity between space and cover, Gaudí favoured comparison, the figure of an embodiment of the tradition in which he was immersed.

In other words, his sense of the sacred is fed by a positive religion of which he offered his contemporaries the outline of a cathedral that represents the union between heaven and earth, between the solar exterior of the earth and the interior depths, now only perceptible in the chiaroscuro of human potential, of heaven.

This is why he does not hesitate to use not only figurative elements drawn from literature, mythology and Christianity, but also a naturalism that swings unceasingly from the invention of organic relations linking the various architectural elements, in an analogy with nature, to experimentation with their decomposition to the point of abstraction, as seen in a number of components of the Sagrada Familia, and to great effect in the Casa Milà.

Gaudí, therefore, from within the Catholic world and in faithful and patient harmony with that world, rather than pursuing a nexus between religious consciousness and art, persisted in experiencing art as an epiphany of the divine.

At times, the mediation of the images, which he uses profusely, appears forced, lacking the pervasive ascesis that would reveal directly the exactness of the form, expressive of a beauty that is at once spiritual and incarnate, that he had perceived so intensely.

Nevertheless, even in these difficult passages, he shows us that which the theological culture of his time had not yet grasped: the urgent need, perceived by contemporary mankind and by he himself first of all, of attaining the divine through the senses, in the flesh, and in the joy of the created world and of art.

His genius allowed him discern an openness that Catholic thought would arrive at, slowly and arduously, much later.

In this sense, Roberto Pane's view seems most perceptive, when he says that the Catalan architect's works had on him the effect of a "a great temptation: to experience just how much truth there is in the concept that art is configured as the living image of freedom, in its ability to take in forms that are not only quite distinct from one another, but go so far as to deny any possibility of reconciliation between them".[9]

As we have seen, this image of freedom has had a substantial impact on the historiography of contemporary architecture, carrying it forward to a categorisation less burdened with preconceptions and, above all, more open, in spite of itself, to the sacred and sanctified.

1 G.R. Collins, *Antonio Gaudí*, Milan, 1960, p. 9. In my brief introduction to Bergós' work, I do not intend to reiterate, either conclusively or with rigorous references to sources, the long and complex trajectory of contemporary criticism. More simply, I should like to trace, at least synthetically, a line through the common ground shared by a considerable number of scholars who are well aware of the influence of Gaudí's architecture not only on the creativity of the architects of our times, but also on the historiography of modernity.

2 Ibid., p. 34.

3 A. Marì, *Euforiòn - Espíritu y naturaleza del genio*, Madrid, 1989.

4 M. Ragon, Historia de la arquitectura y de la urbanística modernas, Rome, 1974, Vol. I, pp. 266-67.

5 Ibid.

6 P. Sequeri, *La belleza necesita forma*, in AA.VV., *Huellas de la Iglesia en la ciudad*, minutes of the Novaro Convention, May 16 1998, published in no. 161-162, July-October edition of the international theological and cultural review "Comunio".

7 H. U. von Balthasar, *Gloria*, Vol. I, Milan, 1971, p. 101.

8 F. Pujols, *La visió artística i religiosa d'En Gaudí*, Barcelona, 1996.

9 R. Pane, *Gaudí*, Milan, 1960, p. 20.

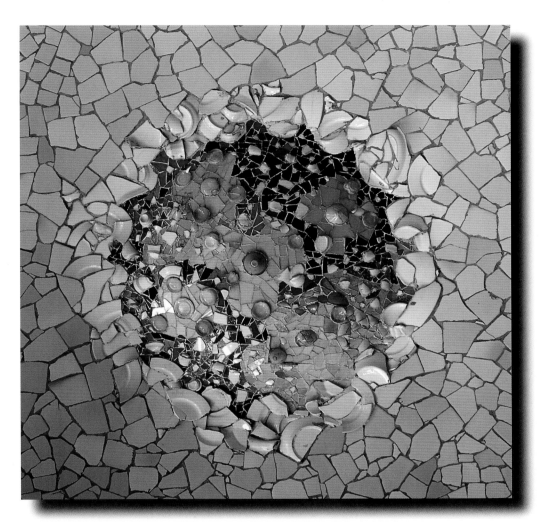

FORMATIVE YEARS

THE CHILD

The Gaudí Family

SOMETIME NEAR THE BEGINNING OF THE 17TH CENTURY, A FRENCH trader from the Auvergne by the name of Gaudí married and settled at Riudoms; six generations later, we arrive at Gaudí's father, whose forebears included seven coppersmiths, one weaver and various farmers. He specialised in the most difficult of the coppersmith's arts, the production of alcohol stills (for "burning wine", as the people of the area say). This skilled and respectable artisan from Riudoms, Francisco Gaudí Serra, married Antonia Cornet Bertrán, from Reus, and together they had five children. Of the five, Francisco, who became a doctor, Antonio and Rosa survived to adulthood.

In central Europe, we find a Gaüdí in Hamburg and a Gaudy in Rohrschach (Switzerland), curiously enough, both of them also architects.

Gaudí's lineage therefore has deep, if distant, roots in Central Europe, mixed with the virtues traditionally found among the country people of Tarragona, a typically Mediterranean people, passionate, industrious, courageous in the face of adversity and somewhat inclined to irony. Gaudí, who identified strongly with these qualities, defended his surnames as thoroughly Catalan: "gaudins" – he would tell me – were medieval advocates and "cornet" is the diminutive of "cuerno" (horn) – and he would react vehemently to any suggestion that his fine features, rosy complexion, pale blue eyes and reddish blonde hair gave him a Nordic look. Once, when the poet Carner made ironic reference to the subject, Gaudí replied that Phidias' Minerva had pale emerald eyes and golden hair.

Birth

On the morning of June 25th, 1852, Antonio Gaudí came into the world in the Campo de Tarragona, a windy corner of the more arid part of Catalonia, where the air is clear, colours are luminous and outlines are sharply drawn, where the images that meet the eye are distinct and tranquil.

He always maintained that he was born in Riudoms, at the "Mas de la Calderería", located exactly halfway between the village and Reus.

The next day, he was taken to be baptised at the parish church of San Pedro, in Reus, where his grandmother lived. The new-born was given the name of his mother and his maternal grandfather.

He had a difficult infancy and was weaned late.

Mas de Calderera farmhouse in Riudoms. This is where Gaudí first saw the light of day, and was his favourite spot on earth.

School Years

The Gaudí family moved to Reus and young Antonio began his education at the infant school run by Master Berenguer, in a garret, and later continued at Mr. Palau's school, although with many interruptions, since before he was six he began suffering from attacks of rheumatism, which were to recur occasionally throughout his life. The boy's education was seriously affected by this illness: he had to spend long periods at the country house, where, as he later recalled, he was often obliged to go mounted on a burro because it was too painful for him to walk.

During these childhood stays at the country house, with its cheerful flowering plants in pots and surrounded by vineyards and olive groves, busy with the clucking of hens, the chirping of songbirds and the buzzing of bees and with the hills of Prades in the background, young Gaudí was impressed by the purest and most pleasurable images of nature, the nature that he always called his "teacher", and he continued to evoke them contentedly in his old age.

Another consequence of his weakened health was that he often had to miss out on his friends' games, a circumstance that favoured his observant nature. Thus, once when his teacher was explaining that birds have wings to fly with, young Gaudí interrupted him, saying

"On our farm the chickens have very big wings but they can't fly; they just use them to run faster." The teacher was taken aback and did not know how to defend his hasty generalisation.

He liked to get out of the city and whenever he was well enough, he would go for short rambles, often to visit the ruins of the Roman kilns on the road to Monterols, or the "Els Capellans" aqueduct.

THE ADOLESCENT

A New Life

At the age of eleven, he began his secondary education at the school run by the Piarist order in Reus, where he did not get especially good grades until his third year. With puberty, his intellectual skills improved considerably and he applied himself well to his studies, getting excellent grades in Geometry and good grades in his other courses, except Religion and Church History, where his grades were only average.

Hikes

His physical condition also improved markedly and he liked to go hiking often with his friends. This not only allowed him to renew his contact with nature but also to get to know the country and he was later to evoke some of its features in his most original works. He also began to take an interest in the more outstanding and varied examples of monumental architecture with which the province of Tarragona is so richly endowed.

Artistic Precocity

At this time he also began showing signs of artistic talent. He illustrated a hand-written weekly school newsletter and designed stage settings for theatre productions presented at the school. After several visits to Poblet, he and his companions Eduardo Toda and José Ribera conceived a project for restoring the monastery. While his friends' motives were patriotic and literary, in tune with the Romantic current of the times, Gaudí was moved more by aesthetic considerations. During his last year of secondary school, he actually drew up plans for the reconstruction project that they had conceived together.

THE YOUNG MAN

Higher Studies and Fruitful Pastimes

At the age of sixteen, he moved to Barcelona to take the last year of secondary school and then begin preparation for his university studies, to which he dedicated five years. He was only able to obtain passing grades and he even failed Rational Mechanics, a subject that, like Analytic Geometry, caused him endless torment on account of its abstract nature. "For all my attempts at concentrating on these studies, a deep-seated preoccupation drove me to dwell on the stability of buildings." Thus, he began to glimpse the forms of equilibrium that he was later to experiment with and quite unexpectedly give shape to. He added, "I did not even dare to express these thoughts to my fellow students because I was convinced that they would not believe me."

He was almost twenty-two when he entered the School of Architecture, after passing his secondary and university courses, along with a course in architectural drafting. The abstract nature of the subjects taught there made them increasingly unappealing to him and he delved further into his own meditations on humanity's great building achievements and particularly on the construction methods that made the enormous monuments of antiqui-

Torras i Bages in the company of Francisco Gaudí and Rosa Egea (Gaudí's father and niece). Drawing by Opisso, dating from c. 1893.

ty possible, on the static characteristics of different building styles, and other considerations, and it was only if, by chance, some explanation related to these architectural cogitations was being given that Gaudí remained spiritually in class. If not, he would be far away, as was usually the case.

This approach resulted in thoroughly justifiable failing grades, which he always accepted as being quite deserved. He once explained to me the ease with which he obtained failing grades on his projects. One examination question required him to design a cemetery gateway and since he was unable to conceive the project without the surroundings that determined its form, he began by drawing the approach to the cemetery, with people in mourning getting out of an automobile, a backdrop of cypress trees and a dim sky with grey clouds. He thus created conditions of lighting and suitable surroundings in which to situate the required gateway and giving an impression of its dimensions. At this point, the professor told him to stop because that was not the way to begin a project. Gaudí, though, could not conceive of any other way to begin, so he left the class and failed the examination, while other fellow students passed it with good grades on the basis of advice that he had given them.

On another occasion, he explained to me how he had passed, somewhat indirectly, his beloved subject of mechanics. While his studies dragged on, thanks to his repeated failures, he worked as an assistant to the master builder Fontserè, who was planning a waterfall for the Ciudadela park. He came across a diagram for a water tank supplying the system which would have collapsed and he calculated an overall static solution for the tank and its supports. Professor Torras, who was a close friend of Fontserè, saw his mechanical study one day and asked who had done it. He was surprised to find that the person responsible was a student of his that he had barely taken any notice of. When it came time for the Mechanics examination, Gaudí had not studied the material presented in Professor Torras' course, but the professor had a strong sense of responsibility and he gave him a passing mark, on the strength of his calculations for the tank supplying the waterfall in the park.

When the specialised library of Architecture began taking shape, Gaudí undertook the most painstaking documentary study that the School had ever witnessed, guided by his eagerness to know more about outstanding constructions and especially by his search for solutions to his mental constructs, most of which, by that time, had led to unsolved question marks. When the first photographs of Greco-Roman, Roman and Byzantine works began to replace engravings, his enthusiasm grew and he would often spend hours poring over, comparing and drinking in these marvels that he had only been able to study previously with the regret caused by seeing them so inaccurately depicted. When he explained all this to me, his exact words were: "I was in heaven."

At the head of the works that he listed as having studied with the greatest interest was Viollet le Duc's *Dictionary of Architecture*, which was at that time the standard handbook of the Romantic architects. He borrowed a copy of this work from his friend Cabanyes and later returned it with pages falling out and full of notes and sketches completing or rectifying the author's ideas. He also studied Viollet's *Dictionary of French Furniture*.

Other French books on medieval decoration and carpentry, as well as *La carpintería de lo blanco*, by López de Arenas, also attracted his attention. He was especially interested in the ingenious designs of Mudejar tracery, saying that they were the fruit of Alexandrian geometry, which the Arabs had simply disseminated.

Although he took his studies much more seriously than his fellow students, Gaudí was affable and attentive with them, he enjoyed their jokes and he was a clever trickster and joker himself, although never with least hint of satirical intent.

Gaudí smoking a cigar, with his father (centre), his niece and Dr. Santaló.

Complementary Studies

Well in advance of the modern concept of History of Art, Gaudí understood that the birth of different styles was not just a result of aesthetic ideas, but that they were linked to the political configuration, the social circumstances and the prosperity of the peoples that produced them. Thus, he dedicated a large part of his extracurricular activities to the study of History and Economy and he attended the Aesthetics classes given by Milà i Fontanals and the Philosophy classes given by Llorens i Barba.

This is a reflection of his characteristic drive to tie up loose ends, to achieve luminous syntheses of the crowning achievements of History and Art.

Added to this dedication to his professional training, his love of classical literature, Shakespearean theatre and the works of the Spanish *Siglo de oro* – from which I often heard him quote – and his enthusiasm for the theatre and especially concerts, shows us just how great a wealth of knowledge he had amassed by the time he finished his studies.

He later also took a great interest in maritime and aerial navigation and in the problems of military strategy, biology and medicine.

Archaeological Visits

He participated assiduously in the visits to the city's monuments and the archaeological outings organised by the architect Elias Rogent, the Dean of the School, and he continued those visits even after he had completed his studies.

During these outings, he would carry on lively discussions on architecture with his fellow students, particularly on the subject of Gothic styles. He was already at that time in favour of modifying the presbytery of the cathedral of Barcelona, with the elimination of the altarpiece that was removed in 1968.

His personal visits to monuments in the rest of Catalonia and the south of France sharpened Gaudí's critical bent and rounded out his artistic knowledge.

Professional Experience

The modest financial circumstances of Gaudí's parents obliged them to sell some of his mother's property to pay for his studies in Barcelona. As a student, he was known for his simple clothing, he borrowed books from his fellow students and already in his first year of Architecture, he was working for the architect Francisco P. del Villar, a Professor at the School, who must have discerned his student's exceptional talent, and for the master builder mentioned earlier. His fellow students believed that he used his income from this work to help his parents financially.

We see, then, that the future architect made an early start in accumulating professional experience, a fact that must have helped make his initial efforts as an architect somewhat easier. Even in his earliest works he showed a complete mastery of the skills required for building and even made original improvements to them.

Gaudí's family tree, drawn up by J.M. Armengol, based on baptismal inscriptions from various parish records.

GAUDÍ'S PERSONALITY

THE MAN

ALL TOO OFTEN, GREAT ARTISTS HAVE BEEN MEDIOCRE INDIVIDUALS, lacking common sense, or worse yet, deplorable individuals, lacking ethics. Gaudí's artistic genius, however, was backed by a highly principled character.

Faith changed the passionate, impetuous, irascible youth into a serene, balanced, exemplary man, who only on rare occasions gave vent to any temperamental outburst and who radiated such a beneficent aura that he sometimes inspired conversion and even heroic sacrifice in those whose lives he touched. He was a man who meditated profoundly on the problems of art and life, whose actions were strictly consistent with his views, who remained absolutely faithful to his deeply held religious convictions, his noble public spirit and his refined aesthetic ideals, and who showed that the highest artistic inspiration is the reward of hard, continuous, slow, methodical and disciplined work.

The young architect, with his attractive good looks and manner, was of medium height and sturdy build. The colour of his eyes, hair and complexion gave him a rather Nordic look, as mentioned earlier, while his broad and prominent forehead, the high and thick bridge of his nose and his wide cheekbones were typically Mediterranean. He did not gesticulate when he spoke, but when he found a subject particularly exciting, his features would liven and his sharp and penetrating gaze would brighten.

Opposing Qualities

Gaudí had a prodigious imagination that allowed him not only to hold forms in his mind with ease, but also to visualise space and construct an over-all conception of whatever it was he was contemplating, distinguishing effortlessly between what was essential and what was accessory. He believed that he had inherited this gift from the coppersmiths on his father's side of the family, whose craft involved creating forms directly in space. This exceptional skill, for which he said he thanked God daily, was damped sufficiently by his sense of moderation to keep him from being carried away by flights of fancy.

His acute intelligence endowed him with an extraordinary capacity for attention and however many digressions and interpolations might come up in conversation, he would always come back to the main subject. At work, his concentration on the matter at hand never seemed to be thrown off by interruptions, noise or the questions of his collaborators. However, this inward concentration was balanced with action, manifest in practical experiments with the results of his mental efforts. He summed up this approach thus: "One must alternate between reflection and action, which are complementary and serve to correct each other" and "In order to move forward, you need to use both legs: action and reflection".

His enthusiasm and his fervour, guided by his intellect, made him tenacious, but his self-criticism led him to proceed calmly and even slowly.

Our architect's genius was surely the product of the co-existence of these opposing qualities, so seldom found in the human character; he was endowed with the typically Nordic, almost Cartesian, qualities of logic and discipline, along with the typically Mediterranean clarity of vision and the passionate imagination characteristic of inspired minds, with the combination giving rise to Gaudí's brilliance.

This double array of complementary qualities was crowned by the most precious of gifts: the lofty sentiments and nobility shining so clearly through his patriotism and devoutness.

The Thinker

Gaudí said that art is made by man for man and therefore must be rational. He gave all of his creations very careful thought and thoroughly deplored cubism in all its varying styles as dehumanising art. He detested the first attempts at abstract art for their lack of plasticity.

He would habitually reason out everything that he saw or studied, everything that he came into contact with and everything that he intuited or imagined.

He argued that no one is useless and that anyone in a postion of responsibility must be aware of the capabilities of the people that they command. He made the following distinction:

Good-living, epicurean Gaudí at the age of thirty-five. Distinguished, elegant, a gourmet, he enjoyed horse-riding, drama and music.

"There are two types of people: temporal and spatial. Anyone who has problems handling numbers will also have difficulty learning music or languages, because they are all linked to time." Thus, once when we had to select a guide for the visitors to the site of the Sagrada Familia, he chose a person who, aside from speaking several languages, also played the violin moderately well. He said that this indicated that they would have a better a command of those languages.

He saw the need to consider every detail of a project and foresee every difficulty that it might present, since laziness is more intellectual than material and the master builder should never count on their workmen to take the trouble to think.

He also came to distrust books thoroughly and he was quick to pick out their inaccuracies, errors and falsehoods. As he often said: "You seldom find what you're looking for in books, and when you do, it's usually wrong." In the end, he always ended up thinking things out for himself.

When rumours began circulating that Barcelona's School of Architecture would be closed, he was prepared to found a private School and he was convinced that it would be successful in attracting people from all over the world. He would have placed his solidly based theories and his talent for teaching and psychology at the service of education and, he added, we would have done nothing as an architect. He was thus full of praise for true teachers, whose vocation leads them to sacrifice their own work in favour of spreading knowledge.

His intellect was not only capable of getting to the heart of a question, it was capable of doing so at great speed. He was able to come up with the correct answers quickly and as was only natural, he set great store by this intellectual agility and would say "I can think of everything that St. Thomas could think of, but in my case, it would take centuries."

He like to compare the clarity of the Mediterranean philosophers with the mists of their Nordic counterparts: "Descartes' basic affirmation loses its clarity as it moves northward. The syllogism 'I think, therefore I am' is the most illogical statement that can be conceived; it would be much more logical to say 'I think, therefore I do not know'. The Mediterranean philosophers go no further than the "I", because it in itself implies existence. This obfuscation was heaviest in Kant (who was from Königsberg, near Russia) and it is the same obfuscation that permeates the nihilists and Bolsheviks."

In spite of his intellectual capacity, he felt the limitations of human intelligence: "Man's intelligence can only act in one plane, with two dimensions. He can solve equations with one unknown, of the first degree. The angels' intelligence is three dimensional, acting directly in space. Man cannot act until he has been presented with the whole fact: at the outset, he can only follow paths, lines on a plane."

He could not tolerate the idea of anyone using their intelligence in the service of falsehood: "Thought is not free, it is subservient to the truth. Freedom is not a quality of thought, but of the will." He also added: "The love of truth must come before any other love."

His keen intelligence and his ability to concentrate intensely provided him with an intuitive grasp of nature and of historical monuments and he often discerned in these monuments functions that had long been forgotten and have since been confirmed through archaeological and archival studies.

The Sensible Man

One consistent quality that is to be found in all of the fields of Gaudí's activities and in all of the directions that he took during his lifetime is that of constant progress and improvement: "One cannot leave out any of the steps, neither the highest nor the lowest one. One must always climb, step by step, in intelligence, virtue, strength ...." He applied Ignatius Loyola's rule of constant effort, which he summed up as follows: "Man must always add to what he already is."

Although he was an avid conversationalist, he was averse to idle chat and empty words: "The only people who are entitled to say foolish things are fools." If it became apparent to him that his listeners were unable to follow his discourse because of their lack of understanding, or because they were distracted or tired, he would stop short and dismiss them with an abrupt "goodbye". He liked to argue and convince others without pressuring them, but he always avoided disputes: "Disputes do not serve to shed light; they merely feed one's pride."

Flattery and adulation annoyed him: "Adulators cannot trusted, because their flattery is meant to deceive." Nor did he tolerate exaggerated courtesy: "Excessive courtesy is rude."

Desk from Gaudí's office.

He once warned a workman not to walk too near a horse, that it was not to be trusted in spite of its docile appearance, because "beasts can be beastly".

He was unselfish by nature and often forgot to present the bill for his work and to pay the people who worked for him. When his father moved to Barcelona, he had to take charge of his son's finances and Gaudí enjoyed asking him for pocket money, as he had done as a child. "One ought to keep their love of money well under control; I am sadly lacking in this. Tasks that give pleasure should not be done for reward. Nothing is gained without some sacrifice and sacrifice means giving of oneself, without reward. This goes for all those who would make their work depend on how much they are paid for it."

Gaudí praised the spiritual worth of poverty and its rewards, even in material terms, at times: "Poverty preserves and protects things." On the other hand, he criticised an excess of generosity in those who cannot afford it, paraphrasing Cambó: "Largesse is a virtue of the rich and a vice of the poor."

He was strong-willed and decisive and placed a great deal of value on character: "Worth is determined more by will than by intelligence. When temperament and talent are balanced, they provide character. A person's talent is often dominated by their temperament and as a result, they are incapable of doing things right."

In Gaudí's opinion, adversity was no excuse for inaction and did not justify failure: "One must act according to circumstances; when the situation is propitious, one should adapt, and when the situation is adverse, one should rebel. All circumstances are helpful because effort is never wasted. Circumstances are a manifestation of providence."

Aside from his enthusiasm for hiking, he liked to ride horses in his free time, but when his increasingly heavy workload no longer left him enough leisure time, he made sure nevertheless that he got sufficient physical exercise. In a play on words, he quipped: "The feet support the head. Walking is an invaluable counterbalance to intellectual effort and is conducive to deep and restorative sleep. A person should keep busy, both mentally and physically, all day, walking and taking exercise, in keeping with their abilities. Then, they will sleep all night and this is equilibrium, compensation, life itself. I have come to the conclusion that one must walk about ten kilometres every day and that this exercise is even more beneficial if it is not done exclusively on level ground. We always go for a walk on the breakwater on our days off and I walk up to Parque Güell, where I sleep, every night." Even before moving there, he observed the traditional habit of a long walk after supper, usually in the company of his close friend Dr. Santaló. When his work no longer left him time for these walks, he would compensate by standing while working or receiving visitors.

His father became a naturist, observing the principles devised by Father Kneipp, and took hydrotherapy treatment for his varicose veins, which succeeded where standard medicine had failed. Impressed by the system's results, Gaudí himself adopted some of its practices. Even in midwinter, he would bathe in cold water and then dry himself with a brisk rub-down, which served as massage and exercise at the same time. He also made a point of vigorously rubbing his eyes, those privileged organs, one of which was far-sighted and the other near-sighted. One of his friends, an oculist, had a monocle made up for him to correct this imbalance, being of the opinion that such a great difference was scientifically unacceptable, but Gaudí found that this artificial equilibrium reduced his field of vision and he stopped using the monocle. He slept with the balcony windows of his bedroom wide open year round and was such a deep sleeper that even the heaviest storms and loudest thunderclaps would not awaken him. For his workshop at the Sagrada Família, he devised an adjustable canopy with counterweights to allow him to work outdoors in the sunshine, calling this workshop his "suntrap".

As a young man, he liked to dress stylishly and elegantly and his everyday apparel included a top hat, morning coat and ankle boots. Later in life, he began eliminating superfluous elements and simplified his dress, even going so far as doing away with underwear and wearing the same suit every day, year-round. When it finally became absolutely necessary to replace his suit, he would send his assistant Sugranyes to have a new one made and Sugranyes had to take an old suit along with him so that the tailor could cut it to the right size.

In his younger years, Gaudí had been a gourmet, but never a gourmand. As he grew older, first in keeping with his naturist convictions, later as a means of therapy for his occasionally recurring bouts of rheumatism and finally out of asceticism, he became extraordinarily frugal in his eating habits. One day, while we strolling on the breakwater, he became so hungry that he had a snack, consisting of a few raw almonds, saying to me: "I am always hungry. I have never

Joan Maragall (1860-1911). Poet and publicist of the Church of the Holy Family (Sagrada Família), his first writings on it date from the year 1900, in a beautiful article entitled "The Temple Being Born".

got up from the table completely full." He criticised those who eat to excess as oversized people who waste their energy and endanger their health. "One must eat to live, not live to eat." Later, fearing that any sort of physical exuberance was detrimental to spiritual well-being, he paraphrased the classical saying: "One must eat and sleep just enough to subsist."

He maintained that salads, of lettuce or curly endive, were the simplest and best way of eating naturally emulsified oil, that it is not true that milk in combination with fruit, even citrus fruits, is indigestible, but that just the opposite is true, and that eating unpeeled fruit is the best way of maintaining the digestive system in good working order. He never drank with his meals and always ate bread with them, even when they consisted of nothing more than nuts and dried fruit. He always finished off with a little bread without a crust, as a sponge for cleaning his teeth, and then a sip of water, which he would swirl around in his mouth for a moment before swallowing it.

He said that abstinence from stimulants and spices heightened his senses and allowed him to appreciate the subtlest aromas and flavours. He also said the most exquisite thing that had ever tasted were freshly picked apricots, that they were a sublime combination of aroma and flavour and that it was impossible to preserve these qualities for long. He was able to tell if fruit had been stored for any length of time, even in a refrigerator, because it lacked any aroma and its flavour was diminished. When he did not have any fresh fruit at hand, he would eat a little honey on bread. He never ate sugar.

Once, when he was already quite old, after having overexerted himself by participating in the Corpus Christi procession, he was bedridden for several days in pain; until that time, I had never seen him ill. Until the end of his life, he maintained all of his mental faculties, his rosy complexion, his alertness, his childlike and shining eyes and all of his strong, white teeth, as the Bible says of the Great Lawgiver.

The Citizen

He shared all of the concerns and ideals that pervaded the dynamic intellectual atmosphere during his youth, along with the poets Verdaguer and Maragall, the clergymen Torras i Bages and Jaume Collell, the writers Ruyra and Carner, the architect Joan Martorell and the Llimona brothers, among other leading lights of the Catalan *Renaixença*, and he was on cordial terms with all them.

In spite of the introverted and isolated nature of his working life, Gaudí was intensely interested in public affairs and avidly followed developments on the political scene. "I am very like my father. At one point, not long before he died, there had just been elections, and he still had enough enthusiasm for the subject to ask me to tell him which candidates had been elected." He railed against separatism and he defended energetically the ideals of regionalism and a strong and united Spain, as conceived by Cambó. He thus felt a great deal of affinity with the Regionalist League, but he never joined any political party.

His ardent patriotism, his controversial talent and his intense interest in politics led Prat de la Riba and Cambó to encourage him to run as a candidate for election to the Town Council or parliament, but Gaudí refused. He justified this stance, saying: "A politician must necessarily have a passion for public affairs and enormous will-power to keep that passion effectively under control. I undoubtedly have that passion, but I am totally lacking that will-power." And he added: "Everyone must use the gifts that God has given them. This is the greatest social perfection that we can aspire to. I am working for Catalonia in my own field, raising its Temple, since a temple is a people's worthiest representation." Over the entry to the Botines house, in León, which was home to a business founded by Catalans, Gaudí placed a beautiful statue of St. George and he used the plaster model for that sculpture to preside the Sagrada Familia's parochial schools, saying: "In this way, the children will learn to commend themselves to our patron saint."

In spite of everything, he admitted that the Catalan people lack a sense of politics. "Catalonia is held back by its envy. This envy is a stumbling block to prosperity, as in the case of other Mediterranean peoples, who have been overtaken by other less talented but more united peoples."

Gaudí possessed an exemplary and valiant civil-mindedness. During times of general strikes and civil unrest, he steadfastly maintained his normal activity, saying: "We must not con-

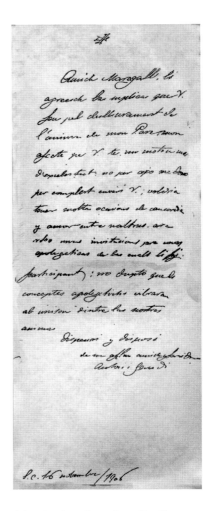

A hand-written letter from Gaudí to Maragall.

Painting of Antonio Gaudí, now in the Gallery of Famous Catalans in the Barcelona's Royal Academy of Letters. Painted by Francisco Domingo.

tribute to disruption by leaving off our normal activity and our work." At times, he would walk out in the street while gun battles were going on, and when someone told him that he should not, he replied: "Bullets don't have addresses on them like letters."

With his accustomed clarity, he made the following distinction: "Governments are always in the hands of one person. Democracy may influence the person in charge, one way or the other, but it will never rule. Governing requires foresight and not compromise, because that leads from abuse to abandonment."

He was of the opinion that the opposition helps to ensure good government: "In order to make safe progress, you need both feet, not lifting one until the other is firmly on the ground. Otherwise, instead of advancing purposefully, we would simply leap about uncontrolledly and then fall. In this same way, governments require an opposition."

He predicted, ten years in advance, the fall of the monarchy and he only believed in dictatorships as a brief and temporary situation: "As good as a dictatorship's intentions may be and for all of their laudable works – and this is being overly generous – it can never be more than a bridge and bridges are meant to be crossed, not lived on. The longer it takes to cross them, the greater the problems that will have to be dealt with on the other side."

He had lived through the disorders of the Carlist Wars and believed that: "War, offering violence as a solution to any problem, is inevitably demoralising. The Crusades were a failure and many sensible Carlists abandoned that cause in the face of the behaviour of the Carlist forces."

His most unpleasant memories of the first attempt at establishing a republic led him to judge the supporters of this form of government very harshly and he did not hesitate to address their leaders in the following manner: "When you republicans are in the opposition, you always make a good impression, because all you have to do is complain, but when you are in power, you do nothing but make stupid mistakes and contradict your own theories."

He especially distrusted the involvement of elementary school teachers in politics: "Elementary school teachers, being accustomed as they are to the partial and warped view of things that they use to make them accessible to children, are fearsome in any context outside their own profession and especially when they get involved in politics."

When discussion turned to the problem of emigration, he pointed out that regulatory provisions were less effective than the preservation and propagation of legal tradition, which would automatically mitigate that problem.

"The institution of the *hereu*1 is necessary in order to preserve the family and its property. In the north of Spain, there is no hereu, but instead the family property is divided equally among the heirs and in the case of numerous families, the family property is broken up into such small portions that none of them can support a family, and this is what makes it necessary for the people to emigrate. Large properties are able to hold large families, as long as they are sufficiently prosperous to provide them with everything that they need."

He was in favour of individual development through culture and the arts and of a high standard of living for the resolution of the so-called social question: "Any solution that does not involve individual improvement, on all levels, is mere talk. I do not believe in the masses or in action in favour of the masses as such. I believe in individual action. There are two great institutions in Barcelona whose importance is poorly understood, even by the people who created them: the *Orfeó Catalá* and the *Institut de Cultura y Biblioteca Popular de la Dona*. Millet and Mrs. Bonnemaison, the widow of Verdaguer i Callis, have done more good than many pious organisations and than all of the socialists put together." In his youth, however, he had been caught up in the socialist movement, which had started in England, and he contributed greatly to the promotion of the textile co-operative, *La Obrera Mataronense*. He soon became disillusioned, though: "Unions and co-operatives, except for commercial ones that have a captive market, are all doomed to failure, because they have no one responsible person in charge and instead a lot of different people who all want to be in charge at once. Or, when they do have one leader, and things go badly, they blame their failure entirely on their leader. In other words, it is just like in the fable of the human body, where the limbs go on strike against the head because they feel that the head is the only part that does no work and, even worse, gives orders to the rest of the body to do all of the work."

He therefore distrusted the sentimental clustering of multitudes and the lack of sophistication of leaderless collectives: "Whether they are proclaimed or not, if collectives do not have someone to direct them, they are only capable of unworthy actions. All collectives involve compromise; since they are driven by what their component parts have in common, and the more component parts a collective has, the lower this common denominator is, and this means that the spirit of a collective is inferior to the spirit of its component parts. Only communities that are subject to a rule and that require sacrifice on the part of their members can provide an improvement on the life of the individual. Collectives are driven by sentiment. The balance between sentiment and reflection, which is the crux of life, is only to be found in the individual. Where there are two or more individuals, sentiment takes over. Any group, whether it is a family, an association or a factory, requires a leader, a father, a director or a manager, to maintain that balance."

He criticised agitators for their flawed reasoning and their counterproductive methods: "Those who stir up the working masses subject them to a succession of strikes. They say that hunger leads to desperation and thus to revolution. This is false. Hunger leads to destitution and destitution leads to death. Desperation is born of encountering insurmountable obstacles standing in the way of plans that have been nurtured for a long time."

He despised communism as a regression that can only take shape in societies in decadence. "Communism only occurs in decadence. This is what happened in Greece, where it failed miserably, as witnessed by Aristophanes in his ridiculing of the communal black soup doled out to the people." With regard to the Russian experience of communism, he added: "The Bolshevik leaders – Nordics – take an analytical approach and have a fragmentary view of the economic problem that they have tried to solve by placing capital in the hands of the community. Since the community is no one, they have made it irresponsible and that is the cause of its destruction."

Thus, in spite of his religious fervour, Gaudí showed himself to be fair-minded, rejecting any sort of extremism and not fitting actively into any political party. Instead, he was in the habit of pointing out their errors, even when their philosophy and sentiments were similar to his own.

THE ARTIST

Over and above his exceptional faculties and his other fortunate abilities mentioned earlier, he was also gifted with a highly intuitive plastic sensibility, allowing him to develop into an outstanding artist. We could describe him with his very own words: "The great masters are those whose sentiments are served by an exquisite and potent intelligence." His original and innovative spirit rose high above his profound knowledge of the great works of history: "Creation is continuous and never-ending, with man's mediation. Man does not create: he discovers and then builds on his discovery. Those who strive to uncover the laws of nature in order to form new works are collaborating with the Creator. Copyists do not collaborate. Thus, originality consists of returning to the source."

He held a classical concept of art, which he completed in his own terms: "Beauty is the radiance of Truth. Without Truth, there is no art. In order to find the Truth, one must know the beings of creation well."

Thus, Gaudí found in nature the key to artistic renewal. Having progressed beyond Romanticism, he avoided the aberrations of the "Modern Style", which he surpassed with a naturalism that is as profound as it is lyrical. His return to the source, then, does not consist of adopting a primitivist vision, nor even an archaising one, but rather of fulfilling once again man's first and most sublime role, that of projecting his spirit onto nature so that nature, in turn, is captured in a new way in his works.

This is why he found pleasure in listing all of the historical precedents of his discoveries. It strengthened their solidity and left behind them the trail of milestones that had successfully pointed the way.

Gaudí belonged to the great Mediterranean family. He sensed the plasticity of harmonious volumes, modulation and colour. On the privileged shores of our sea, the menhir becomes an obelisk, the tree trunk becomes a Doric column and the clumsy efforts of the East become graceful cupolas. Here, the clarity of the light demands exacting geometrical precision and full corporeality. This is where all of the plastic arts finally take full shape in three dimensions: here, architecture is no longer merely the propagation of sections, sculpture is not limited to profiles and painting is not bound by outlines. Gaudí situated and related the Mediterranean latitude – light and climate – and mentality and contrasted them with all that is not Mediterranean:

Gaudí's signature. The first was done at the age of thirty-three, the second at forty-four, and the last at sixty-six.

"Virtue is to be found where the middle quality occurs; Mediterranean means the middle of the Earth. On its shores, with its medium light at 45 degrees, which is the light that best defines solids and reveals their form, is where the great artistic cultures have flourished, thanks to this balanced light. It is neither excessive nor insufficient, as both of those extremes are blinding and the blind do not see. On the Mediterranean, things are seen clearly and this is necessarily the foundation of true art. Our plastic strength resides in the balance between sentiment and logic. The northern races are obsessive and this obsession smothers sentiment, and the lack of light engenders spectres. With the southern races, the overly strong light leads them to neglect rationality and they produce monstrosities. With both dim and blinding light, people see poorly and their spirit is abstract. Mediterranean art will always be clearly superior to Nordic art, because it relies on the observance of nature. At best, the Nordic peoples produce pretty works, but not outstanding ones, this is why they buy Mediterranean works. On the other hand, they are particularly gifted for analysis, science, industry ...."

In the same way as Leonardo da Vinci, whom he greatly admired, Gaudí was part artist and part sage. He believed that the practice of art requires all-round knowledge and he acquired a vast store of it himself. His observations on the great artists of history were always exceedingly precise, but when he spoke of the Greeks of Pericles' time, or of the Lombard builders and Byzantine decorators, or when discussing the works and legends of Sansovino and Cellini (in his opinion, the two greatest artists of the Renaissance), of Titian and El Greco and the Baroque architects, he would become exalted and on more than one occasion I saw his eyes become tearful with emotion.

Like all true innovators, Gaudí was self-taught and could never give rise to a "school". A few of his collaborators and admirers, moved by his presence or dazzled by his splendour, have felt drawn to certain external aspects of the complex art born of his genius, but even in the best of cases, their works have been merely a faint echo of his and in the rest, much inferior to when they simply followed their own modest inspiration. In spite of the fact that he could not have disciples, the revitalising principles of architecture with which he imbued his works will ineluctably mark a glorious and historically fertile juncture.

We should not forget, however, that Gaudí's enormous artistic talent did not keep him from taking part in modest projects, where he cultivated a popular approach, improvisation and even humour.

One other characteristic of this singular man was that he felt himself to be an artist from a very early age, unlike the architect Joan Martorell, the sculptors Meunier and Mallol and so many others who not only did not begin in their youth but did not even realise their true artistic vocation until quite a late age. What is more, his gifts did not decline with age. Quite the contrary, his last works were his greatest and the ones most overflowing with spiritual freshness.

Work and Inspiration

Gaudí was an indefatigable perfectionist. In spite of his exceptional artistic intuition, he was never satisfied until he could be absolutely sure on the basis of experiments and severe self-criticism. When a group of architects who were visiting the façade of his church while it was under construction asked him for a technical explanation, he replied: "Gentlemen, you have studied and you are dismayed at not understanding what I am doing, but I have also studied and I am still studying and working unceasingly." He did not for minute believe in improvisation: "Musical impromptus are no such thing; no one ever improvises." Nor did he trust in inspiration to lighten his workload, but instead he believed that it had to be accepted as a gift: "It is foolish to believe that blessings will rain down upon us without our making every possible effort, as Saint Teresa said."

He was not concerned with the works of others, nor with criticism of his own: "He who has work to do should not criticise the work done by others or bother to defend his own. Instead, he should go about doing his work and criticise it himself in order to refine and improve it."

More out of a desire to facilitate his own research than to save himself work, he always surrounded himself with patient and compliant associates and he never shifted any of his own responsibility onto them, but instead showed them, in an ingenious way, how to go about their work. "A master must make the great sacrifices; his subordinates make the small sacrifices that

The first portrait of Gaudí
to be published in Spain.

are not required of the master. The master must provide the means for carrying out his instructions and make up for anything that is lacking. It is a poor master who complains of the quality of his craftsmen!" He employed the inevitable technique of intelligent repetition to achieve improved solutions: "Everyone makes mistakes, but systematic repetition helps one to make fewer." He pointed out that in the manuscripts of our great poet Verdaguer there are magnificent poems that were recast six or seven times.

The façade of the Palau Güell was completely redrawn twenty-eight times and some of its details changed completely. This was inevitably an exhausting exercise for his assistants, causing Gaudí to complain: "I have tired out those working with me by always trying to improve things, but I have never stopped working on them until I was convinced that they could not be improved any further."

This explains how it was that Gaudí spent several decades on the design of the naves of the Sagrada Familia, whose columns had already taken him four years to perfect, and that he worked for fourteen years on the details of the lanterns crowning the apsidal chapels before he considered them finished. This apparent slowness is reminiscent of Leonardo Da Vinci, who took two years to finish the composition of the Battle of Anghiari, four years from his initial studies until the finished version of the Mona Lisa and sixteen years to prepare the casting of his monumental equestrian statue of the Duke of Sforza. The plastic inspiration and the lofty sentiments of these works, controlled by an exhaustive analysis and born of painstaking search, make them seem to come alive and appear to have sprung effortlessly from the hand of their creator.

It comes as no surprise, then, that Gaudí should reject out of hand works of simple intuition, both those lacking rational refinement and those diminished by an abstraction that overwhelms plasticity and unbalances sentiments. At the exhibition of French art in Barcelona in 1917, walking straight through the halls where *fauve* Cubist and abstract paintings were shown, without stopping, he said to me, glowering, "This is nothing."

A visit by Mgr. Ragonesi, the Papal Nuncio, accompanied by Gaudí (left) and Dr. Reig, Bishop of Barcelona (right) to the Sagrada Familia, when work on the job had come to a halt owing to a shortage of finance. On this occasion, the Nuncio said to the Bishop: "There can be no doubt about it: Mr. Gaudí is the Dante of Architecture, that is how I see him".

The Architect

As the senses are various and varied – "Hearing is less perfect than sight because it requires time" – he proclaimed the spatial arts as more sublime than those involving time, in a paraphrase of St. Paul: "Hearing is the sense of Faith and sight is the sense of Glory, because Glory is the vision of God. Sight is the sense of light, of space, of plasticity; vision is vastitude, it sees what is and what is not."

He explained the kinship of the different spatial arts: "Light is the mother of the plastic arts. Architecture is the measurement and ordering of light; sculpture is the play of light; painting is the portrait of light drawn in colours, which are its separate components." He made an even finer distinction, referring to the structural nature of Architecture and the imitative nature of the others: "Painting, by means of colour, and sculpture, by means form, elaborate existing organisms: figures, trees, fruit ...., expressing their inner essence through their external aspect. Architecture creates organisms and therefore must be governed by a law that is in consonance with the laws of nature; architects who do not observe that law create oddities rather than works of art."

He waxed eloquent in proclaiming the primacy of his preferred art – "Architecture is foremost: *arch* – pre-eminent. All other arts are in need of her: museums, concert halls and performances..." – while also reaffirming its priority as the most social of the arts.

He detailed the order of its qualities, claiming as an error any assessment based on form: "In architecture, form is fourth: first, there is situation; second, measure; third, material; and fourth, form. The sense of touch gives form but it does not situate it; sight not only gives form but also situates it with form, dimension and colour. These four give stability and all of the remaining qualities."

He defined the architect as "The synthetic man, who has a clear vision of an ensemble, before it exists, who situates and combines elements in a plastic relationship and at the exact distance." And he affirmed that this prior intuition comprised the static aspect and the sense of colour.

Finding in the master this elevated concept of architectural synthesis, as going beyond the daunting challenges posed at the artistic level to solve those dealing with mechanics and use and calling into play an extensive grasp of science, technology and other related disci-

The first photograph of Gaudí
to appear in the press
(*L'Art et les Artistes*, Paris, 1908).

plines, we should not be surprised at his affirmations: "Anyone who wishes to practise real architecture must not only possess a special aptitude but must also follow the example of a person who wishes to climb a high mountain: they must take accurate stock of their strength and arm themselves with discipline and even sacrifice, indispensable qualities for anyone hoping to achieve such a lofty goal."

His composition eschews the monotony of the unbroken plane and turns instead to the contrast of retreating and advancing elements, balancing each bright and detailed convexity with the shadow of a simplified concavity.

Already in his first works in collaboration, before becoming an architect, he was creating hyperbolic and trumpet forms and helical encircling elements, such as his father used in making the arms and coils of his stills. He soon also realised that planes do not exist in reality, since walls are not perfectly flat and wooden soffits warp, becoming paraboloid or planoid. He then resolutely adopted this geometric form along with the other two already mentioned, combining them in another of the characteristics of Gaudinian plasticity.

And lastly, one further outstanding feature of his architecture is to be found in the greater continuity of elements that meld, fit together or even fuse, losing their individuality and emphasising the unity of the work, even in its minor details. He criticised the classical arts in this respect: "The erroneous distinction between sustaining and sustained elements gives rise to an incongruous discontinuity between the upright or column and the arch or lintel, with decorative elements used in an attempt to disguise that discontinuity: capitals, corbels, cornices ..." In much the same way and with even greater justification, he criticised medieval builders: "They ornament to hide false structural forms, generally in a barely noticeable way, since elements are repeated industrially with no consideration of proportion or situation."

Gaudí's bent for planning led him unconsciously to expand the utilitarian projects that were proposed to him and he almost always found himself constrained by the material limitations and the lack of spiritual content of these buildings. With the huge plot where the Milà building stands, he wanted to erect one grandiose edifice with a central patio and a double ramp allowing residents to drive automobiles to their flats on the upper floors, but he had to desist and instead build two large blocks of spacious apartments. When he took charge of the construction of the Expiatory Church of the Holy Family, the Sagrada Familia, he was immediately disappointed to find that the work already done was not aligned on the diagonal axis of the block and he boldly extended the naves, with the staircase reaching the adjoining block and covering Calle Mallorca. He was not content until he undertook the definitive project for the Sagrada Familia, a project offering him unlimited possibilities. When he heard that there had been funds left over after the construction of Sacré Coeur at Montmartre was completed, he exclaimed "That would never happen to me."

As a man of his time, he took advantage of all of the resources offered by mechanical science and industry and he put them to use with an admirable sense of practicality. What is more, he used his building materials and architectural elements so appropriately that, without the least deliberate effort in that direction, he became a technical innovator to be reckoned with, to the extent that, paradoxical as it may seem, he was the most influential architect among his contemporaries.

He was the pioneer in the reaction against the use of terrace roofs as single cover, the first to build them in sections and with independent beams; the first of any builders or architects to make reinforced concrete beams; the leader in using balanced arches and vaults with rigorously mechanical axes; the first to reintroduce the cupola-covered halls that are so common today; the restorer of inclined columns; the promoter of double doors; the first to use the Mouras shaft in Barcelona; the one to come up with a pleasing and effective means of ventilation and adjustable lighting for flats; the one to invent a system of tubular bells, electrical lighting for the Sagrada Familia and a method for construction of stained glass windows used in the cathedral of Palma de Mallorca, all of them providing the most outstanding technical solutions for the most complex problems presented by architectural acoustics and optics; the one who found a solution for monumental sculpture, using modelling, armatures, multiple photography and stereoscopy; the only one in the world to achieve a synthesis of stability allowing him to provide our great National Temple with spacious naves with a double stone roof without resorting to buttresses or clusters of columns and isolating the load bearing on each one. If he had had access to pre-stressed concrete for the vaults, or synthetic urea resins for curving wood, or plastics for twisted fixed panels, with what other technical marvels might he have enriched his work!

His love of traditional construction gave him a fondness not only for brick vaulting but also for masonry and rubble work and he called in specialists in these arts from Tarragona and Lérida for some of his projects. He improved construction methods and he remarked, when referring to his special interest in the technology of building: "If I had not been an architect, I would most like to have taken up shipbuilding."

The utilitarian component of his work is never marred by its artistic form nor by its constructive complexity; just the opposite is true. Layout, access, connections between rooms and distribution of services are all excellent, stairs, ramps, banisters, parapets, seats and furnishings are all of exceptional comfort and the placement and form of pulls, handles, grilles, burners, fasteners, etc. is the most convenient for their use. It goes without saying that the dimensions, lighting, ventilation and heating of rooms in his secular buildings are paragons of the humanisation of architecture. He also built in exceptionally effective hiding places to store documents and valuable objects and did not neglect appropriate provisions for keeping watch over and guarding entries against any unwanted intrusion.

Over and above his deep-seated sense of mechanics, he also had a refined sense of construction, which, in his opinion, took precedence over the former. This is manifest in the precise bonds of the ashlars in his astonishing constructions in worked stone, in his bold projections in masonry and brickwork, in his masterful wrought iron work and his numerous artifices for counteracting the movement of wooden elements: reduced width of panels and grooving of their faces, or their complete weakening, using curved forms with supporting ribs, carved decorations with emphasis on the joints of the most mobile pieces, small cuts and perforations to weaken the central fibres of posts, arms and legs of furnishings, diminishing progressively with distance from joints, etc.

In the Calvet house, he built several benches in *melis* pine with seats and backs using mortise and tenon joints and fitted into a frame. Thanks to this most effective joinery, when a bomb exploded in the house opposite, the shock wave reduced the bench nearest the outside door to pieces in such a way that none of them were broken and the bench could be rebuilt without difficulty.

The builders carrying out his constructive contrivances themselves often did not understand his reasoning and did not believe that they would work. Thus, when Gaudí used projecting brick corbels to support corner galleries in the Vicens house, an older construction worker warned the young architect that, when the galleries were added on, their weight would crush the corbels. Gaudí explained to him that the cohesion of the mortar and the built-in counterweights would provide complete stability. The worker was unconvinced and stayed for hours after the work was completed, waiting to see it collapse. It is still standing today. At times, not even his technical assistants were able to grasp the intricate constructive and mechanical concepts that Gaudí had them draw up and one of them admitted that he still did not understand why the pierced groin arches supporting the roofs of the Bellesguard mansion did not crack.

Aside from being a very talented designer, Gaudí was also an extraordinary constructor and an expert foreman, foreseeing even the most minute details and everything required to carry out the project and selecting the most expert workmen for each type of work, rounding off their training in all aspects that went beyond the normal technology used in their trade. The Villa Quijano, in Santander, was built without Gaudí ever visiting the site or even meeting the owner. In spite of the innovations incorporated into the project, it was built without any difficulty.

"Architect also means master builder, the person who directs the work, and as such he is a governor in the purest sense of the word, in that he does not assume a pre-existing constitution, but rather creates one himself. Thus, the greatest governors are known as nation builders." This explains why, whenever he took part directly in the construction of a project, he always carried it even further, to the extent that, in order to have an accurate plan of the construction, it had to be redrawn once the building was finished.

Lastly, another of Gaudí's hallmarks is that he did not conceive of decoration as a cosmetic accessory, added on *a posteriori*, but rather as the external expression that emerges from the essence of the work and provides a beautiful finish for it. This facet of Gaudí merits separate mention.

Gaudí in the street.
Drawn by Joaquín Renart.

The Decorator

Portrait of Gaudí published in
La Esfera. (June 19th, 1926).

We have already mentioned that Gaudí conceived his works complete with their decoration and even their colouring.

Already as a student, he wrote in his diary that he intended to make serious studies of ornamentation and then went on to note down some interesting concepts, which I will transcribe later.

In ornamental reliefs, he based his work on sculptural grounds and produced warped encircling elements, obtaining surprising results. The decoration of the Arab-style pavilions that he built for the Cadiz and Barcelona Expositions of 1887 and 1888 was "especially well-received by the critics". Along the same lines, in the case of the pews and kneelers that he designed for the chapel of the Palacio de Comillas, in Santander, "the craftsmen were astonished by how attractively their work turned out, in comparison with the work that they had done for other architects in the same setting".

Gaudí preferred strictly architectural decoration to any other sort and thus his plastic composition is made complete by its emphasis of its constructive elements, underlining their mechanical function and even their utilitarian aspect. He greatly simplified mouldings and went so far as even to eliminate them altogether when using warped forms, because "paraboloids, hyperboloids and helicoids, with their constant variation of the incidence of light, have their own richness of nuance and do not need any sort of ornamentation or even moulding". Nevertheless, when the liturgical and didactic nature of his work on the Sagrada Familia called for symbolic and figurative representations on an ornamental ground providing them with an appropriate backdrop, he wholeheartedly took up the task of resolving the difficult problems posed by architectural sculpture, not finding any artist specialising in this field at that time.

Gaudí's concept of sculpture is eminently structural and based on the living skeleton. It not only defines posture, but is the basis of the figure's character, since it is the one invariable element. He justified this as a starting point, saying: "A person's character and physiognomy are a consequence of their skeleton. Even if they lose weight, or their skin becomes wrinkled or takes on a different tone because of illness, their distinctive features do not change."

The essential aspect, then, was the shape and situation of the joints and their musculature and he therefore had no qualms about using casts taken directly from live models, a technique that, in spite of its difficulty and inconvenience, was the fastest way of obtaining satisfactorily those basic sculptural elements.

He defended the use of casts, "a technique also used by the Greek masters, such as Lyssipus, the Florentines and some well-known sculptors who are also friends of mine and who would prefer not to have it become generally known that they have employed this system, for fear that their work would then be looked down upon. I find this contempt for the use of casts just as ridiculous as the pedantry of painters and sculptors who do not lower themselves even to referring to models but work only from memory. In fact, Clarassó's best male nude, 'Man digging his own grave' was made from a cast, and there are always casts of hands, feet, knees, etc. to be found in sculptors' studios."

He always chose models that would best represent the person being depicted and for this purpose he made very meticulous studies of the anatomical postures and physiognomies that would most expressively communicate traits and states of mind, quoting examples from busts of classical figures known from history. In the case of animals, he studied them in movement, "because another way of discerning the skeleton is to observe and take notes from a moving model". When he could not obtain live animals, he would insert a wire through their spinal cord, the fundamental part of the skeleton, in order to position them in the desired posture.

On one occasion, he was insistent on using a scorpion and rummaged through the rubble of a vacant plot until he found one. He carefully studied how to capture it without hurting it and took it back to his workshop, showing it to his craftsmen and explaining where he intended to place it. However, in a moment of distraction, he was stung by the scorpion and he threw it to the ground, saying "Because you hurt me, I'm going to leave you out."

The donkey in the depiction of the Flight into Egypt on the façade of the Sagrada Familia was done using a cast. When I asked him how he had managed it, he told me: "We bought an old donkey from a woman who would often come by peddling things. When we found that it would not stand still to let us take the cast, I had it suspended, with a strap under its belly, and when it found itself in mid-air, it became completely calm and we were able to take the cast without difficulty."

After a cast was taken, then came the complicated task of correcting it, because "the softer parts are lost in a cast. I take advantage of this correction to make the modifications that are meant to endow the figure with the character of the person being depicted and, on the visible parts, the simplifications required by the material that will be used for the sculpture itself." The next step was to clothe the parts that were not to remain visible and once the clothing was in place, with the appropriate drapery, it was sprayed with plaster slurry to give it body.

The completed figure was then carefully reproduced by co-ordinates to acquire a model one quarter of the figure's final height, which was greater the higher up it was to be placed. This model was then distorted to compensate for optical effects, with "progressive vertical augmentation and constant horizontal augmentation. To obtain these results, we take the co-ordinates of the correctly proportioned figure using a surrounding armature with uniform scales and then the distorted figure is produced in another armature with adjusted co-ordinates."

"Lastly, this model is then enlarged in plaster to its final size and put in place, so that the finishing corrections can be made as required by lighting and by the surrounding architectural and ornamental elements."

In the diary mentioned earlier, he had already noted: "Decoration always has been and always will be polychrome," and he supported this affirmation taking nature as an example, where none of the various kingdoms shows a monotony of tone. Thus, "Architectural elements demand polychrome, whether total or partial." "The sun is the great painter of the Mediterranean lands," he proclaimed, relying on the patina that light, air and micro-organisms create on the fine materials used in construction. He therefore logically reserved polychrome for the areas less exposed to patination and more protected from the rain. He also used coloured stone and polychrome glazes to cover wall surfaces built with ordinary materials.

In keeping with his habit of citing precedents, he said: "The Greeks stuccoed and painted temples built from coarse stone and they even painted their handsome Pentelic marble, in spite of its nobility and beauty. The Nordics do not have a feeling for colour and they are reluctant to believe that the Parthenon was painted. When they found remains of painted stucco, they made no comment."

He also pointed out that colour is a sign of life: "People are not so easily fooled. When they see someone who is pallid, they say that he looks like a corpse, and when they see a corpse with rosy cheeks, they say that it looks as if it were alive."

Already in his earliest work, he exploited the contrast of red bricks with yellowish masonry, or with the shiny greens and whites of ceramics. He would often offset the cold darkness of wrought iron with bright and attractive stone. He selected yellow, green and black schists to obtain masterful gradations and to contrast active elements and filler.

Later, he covered the whole façade of the Casa Battló with glazed materials in richly varied tones and in the Casa Milà, he went so far as to cover turrets and chimneys with ceramics, meant here to accompany a monumental group depicting an apparition of the Virgin Mary that was to be sculpted in stone with Venetian mosaic and details in gilded metal and coloured glass, crowning the white marble attic. He also expected to see the main mass of the *Pedrera* (Catalan for "quarry", as the Casa Milà is commonly known) complemented by the leaves and flowers of climbing plants grown in pots called for in his plans. Lastly, in his master-work, the Sagrada Familia, he planned for the archivolts of the porticoes, including their flora and fauna decorations, to be painted; as a preliminary study, he had begun to polychrome one of the models. Outside, he used Venetian mosaic for the finials of gable ends and bell towers, and inside, to overlay vaults and parapets, as in the most opulent Latin and Byzantine basilicas.

It was in translucent polychrome that he attained the greatest richness and intensity, taking a fundamentally impressionist approach to the use of tones. On his visit to the south of France, he was profoundly disappointed by the French grisaille stained glass that he saw there, calling it trash, and also criticising harshly its overly heavy contours, since "they make the figures look like caricatures".

The procedure referred to earlier, as novel as it was logical, of creating stained glass windows by layering the three primary colours – and at times also clear glass – in different thicknesses, to obtain light of varying intensity, in the service of his privileged vision, made the magnificent stained glass windows of the cathedral of Palma de Mallorca possible. Of the image of Saint Ferdinand, one of the most outstanding in these incomparable windows, he said: "I challenge anyone to produce, without using the three different glasses, the effect of the setting sun reflecting off of his white horse."

A sketch by Gaudí for the baldachin of the cathedral of Palma de Mallorca.

Gaudí in the cathedral's Corpus Christi procession in 1924, next to the banner of the Sant Lluc Artistic Circle.

The Creative Process

If we imagine the master's natural gifts, his exceptional autodidactic training, his unflagging industriousness and his unwavering faith in his art, all of them at the service of his aesthetic ideals and his inspiration, we can arrive at some idea of how Gaudí's most singular creations were conceived and grew until blossoming into their finished form.

He was able to envisage, almost effortlessly, numerous solutions for the projects proposed to him. He would weigh these different possibilities carefully until he arrived at the one that he considered most appropriate and attractive, seeing it already taking shape in space with all of its essential volumes and even its colours.

Then he would begin preparing the project, slowly, carefully, tenaciously, subjecting himself to his own implacable criticism. In this way, he would ensure that every functional, constructive, mechanical and aesthetic aspect was just right. He would unify this architectural complexity in the synthesis that distinguishes all true works of art. His great admirer, the architect Joan Martorell, fearing that he might ruin one of these masterful creations, advised him not to modify it any further, that in trying to have it all, he would lose it all. When Gaudí told me of this incident, he added "That is the motto of a saint, which he was, but it does not apply to art." He then went on to take the concept to its ultimate expression, with his insatiable desire for simplification and artistic perfection.

This explains the enormous distance between his initial sketches and the final shape of his projects, without the original overall idea being diminished in the slightest.

Gaudí, the perpetually dissatisfied artist, corroborated and improved the work being done, experimenting with models, observing and comparing the results with historical works and even with his own work previous to the project at hand. This approach, which he followed even while construction was in progress, would transform the project as it was being carried out, creating as great a distance or greater between the work actually done and the plans for it, as between the plans and their initial drafts.

The works of architects without an artist's vocation are inferior to their plans for them and the materials that they use lose their value, the more noble ones being diminished and the more humble ones becoming pitiful. Gaudí, however, emphasised magically the unique virtues of each material and achieved an extensive range of expression – in keeping with each one's constructive demands – such that, in enriching his plastic repertoire, it was wholly in keeping with the lively humour so evident in his later works.

THE RELIGIOUS MAN

Gaudí came from a pious family and he received a thorough religious education from the Piarist fathers. The ember of Christianity residing in the deepest part of his spirit was never completely extinguished, although it burned low for close to a decade. It later rekindled and he became a devout Christian, and later still burned even brighter, leading him to asceticism.

When he began working as an architect, he was well-received immediately and earned a comfortable living. The enthusiastic and dynamic Gaudí was caught up in the joy of living and, as mentioned earlier, dressed with impeccable good taste and revelled in creature comforts and was fond of good food, sweets, wine and tobacco. He enjoyed horseback riding and automobile outings, he had season tickets for the Teatro Principal and he was a regular participant in the affable conversational gatherings at the Liceo opera house, although he never took any of these pursuits to extremes. He showed little concern for religious ideas.

One could say that he had taken up Cohelet's somewhat Epicurean maxim: "Man has no well-being under the sun other than to eat, drink and be merry and may these joys accompany his labours all of the days that God grants him on this earth."

The Ways of the Lord

In spite of the tense atmosphere of the times, a result of the pugnacious attitude taken by a substantial part of the clergy – one of the disastrous consequences of the last Carlist war and a source of anticlerical sentiments – Gaudí never allowed himself to be swept along by the general current and no one ever heard him make a derogatory remark about the Church. The Lord had chosen him and began by bringing him into contact with fervent Christians, ones who were cultured and refined.

Shortly after finishing his studies, he began associating with the distinguished gentleman and architect Joan Martorell and worked closely with him on the construction of the Salesian Sisters' convent. Gaudí was impressed by Martorell's practical and noble faith. Years later, recalling their intimate conversations, Martorell's friendly advice and his charitable works, Gaudí exclaimed, "He was a wise man and a saint." He also became friendly with the publisher Bocabella, a profoundly devout man of exceptional culture, under whose influence he conceived and undertook the building of the Sagrada Familia. Bocabella took advantage of his profession to promote popular piety and he published the work *Año Cristiano*, which he presented to Gaudí, giving him his introduction to spiritual literature.

Gaudí also came into contact with distinguished churchmen, such as the Reverend Enrique d'Ossó, founder of the Teresan Sisters order, Bishop Grau and Bishop Morgades, Monsignor Torras i Bages, who later became Bishop of Vic, the leading Jesuit Father Ignacio Casanovas and the Phillipian poet Luis María de Valls.

Gaudí in Barcelona cathedral.
Drawn by Juan Matamala, 1924.

Gaudí was most decisively influenced by his illustrious fellow citizen of Reus, Bautista Grau, the Bishop of Astorga, who was also a legal expert, philosopher, archaeologist and one of the forerunners of the movement for renewal of the Church. Bishop Grau commissioned Gaudí to build the new Episcopal Palace in Astorga to replace to the one that had been destroyed by fire. During the six years taken to complete the building, Gaudí made frequent visits to Astorga and the Bishop instilled in him an enthusiasm for the liturgy. Together, they studied the Bishops' Rite and the Roman Missal and Bishop Grau encouraged him to read daily Dom Guéranger's *L'Année liturgique*, a habit that he maintained for the rest of his life.

By the age of forty, Gaudí was fervently devout and his religious convictions were deeply rooted. Recalling his period of religious indifference, he would say "A man without religion is spiritually handicapped, a disabled man."

At the same time that his religious faith was being re-awakened, he suffered some painful experiences that served to spur this spiritual rebirth. While putting the finishing touches to the decoration of the Casa Vicens, he was inspired by a desire for a home of his own, and expressed that desire in the inscription placed in the centre of the façade: "On the hearth, let the fire of love burn brightly." After pursuing a number flirtations and one unhappy romance, this desire took shape when he was thirty-three in the form of a serious courtship with a very devout young lady who, at the last minute, decided to enter a convent. The bitter lesson of this renunciation of human love in favour of divine love made a profound impression on him and led him to choose for himself a life of exemplary Christian celibacy. He then understood clearly the importance of renunciation and sacrifice: "Life is a battle; in order to fight and win one needs strength and that strength is to be found in virtue, which can only be sustained and grow through the cultivation of the spirit by means of religious observance." "Physical exercise and sobriety of food, drink and rest are mortifications of the body that effectively combat lust, sloth and drunkenness." "Life is love and love is sacrifice. Sacrifice is the only truly fruitful action. The spiritual and material advancement of religious orders proceeds from the sacrifice made by all of their members for the good of the community."

The painful separations and close experiences of the chill of death that he underwent during this period of crisis were undoubtedly a further and persistent encouragement to renounce human ties. A dramatic fall while horseback riding impressed upon him the fragility of life; the death of Vicentó, his construction foreman, in a fall from scaffolding caused Gaudí to weep; and the death of his dear friends Bocabella and Grau, occurring within three years of each other, and his own near brush with death when a stone falling from an overhang came close to crushing him, all led him to meditate deeply on the problems of pain and life after death.: "The idea of death will never separate anyone from God; this is why tombs are in churches. Those who do not lead an upright life do not wish to think of death and that is why they prefer it to be far removed from the Church. Without the thought of death, there can be no good moral or physical life."

He was particularly affected by the death of the Bishop of Astorga. He had a premonition of that death, caused by his perception of the Bishop's aura of heavenliness. "Nobody thought his illness was of any importance, but I saw immediately that he was mortally wounded.... and I said so to those around him. Do you know how I realised that the Bishop was fatally ill? I

Josep M. Bocabella y Verdaguer (1815-1892), founder of the Association of Devotees of St. Joseph.

found him so beautifully transformed that it occurred to me that he could not live. He was beautiful, too beautiful, everything personal about him had disappeared. The lines of his face, his colour, his voice... There was nothing left of his person except something that was totally removed from mundane reality. And perfect beauty cannot live..."

The Liturgist

In the same way that Gaudí heralded the movement of a return of the intellectual elite to spirituality, he was also one of the earliest forerunners of the Church's liturgical renewal. He rightly said: "The history of architecture is the history of the temple." From this stems his interest in functional matters and the sacred arts as an architect, prior to his interest in them as a devout Christian. As mentioned earlier, even as a student he discussed with his fellow students the need to move the Choir of the cathedral of Barcelona, to leave the nave clear for the faithful.

His precise artistic sense allowed him to perceive immediately the imperfection of the lighting, of the inappropriateness of the canticles and of the plastic poverty of the images and altars in use at the time.

As with so many other refined spirits, the liturgy was one of the aspects of religiosity that most attracted him. It has been said or assumed that Gaudí had made a profound study of the liturgy. When Brehier published his interesting book *L'Art chrétien. Développement iconographique des origines à nos jours*, he dedicated its final chapter to Gaudí's masterwork. I showed him a copy and when he saw the author's statement that Gaudí was obviously familiar with the *Summae* and *Speculae* and the medieval treatises on symbolism, he exclaimed: "I haven't read any of those!" He had learned the living liturgy by following the Church's yearly cycle through the fifteen volumes of Dom Guéranger's dense opus and he had replaced his paperback copy with the hardback edition, so that he could read it in the dim light of the cathedral and so that he could hold it open and even folded back on itself. The covers of these volumes were blackened with use and their pages mended with adhesive paper and strips of canvas.

"*Sapientia*, wisdom, is derived from *sapere*, to taste." In order to better savour the liturgical texts that he read in French, he took advantage of the presence of a relative that Torras i Bages had sent to keep him company during his convalescence from Malta fever in Puigcerdà to improve his command of Latin. Thus, in his later years he no longer carried the heavy tomes of *L'Année liturgique* with him to church, just a small pocket edition *Roman Missal*. After a pontifical service officiated by the Papal Nuncio, he said to me: "Did you hear how he pronounced the Latin? It was sheer delight!"

When Doctor Campins commissioned Gaudí to take charge of restoration of the cathedral of Palma de Mallorca, he did not study the liturgical treatises that were then beginning to be published with guidelines, but instead, following his own experimental approach, he spent a year observing and noting down all of the defects that the inappropriate placing of liturgical furnishings caused in the performance of episcopal rites, diminishing their significance and splendour.

He was taken by the Church's role as builder: "The Church never stops building and this is why its head is the Pontiff, which means builder of bridges. Temples are bridges to glory."

He also admired the Church's exquisite touch in the use of all styles and in receiving the homage of all of the arts. "The Church makes use of all of the arts, both those involving space (architecture, sculpture, painting, metalwork ...) and those involving time (poetry, song, music ...); the liturgy offers us lessons in aesthetic refinement." Nevertheless, one incident in Astorga demonstrated to him that the Church's spiritual order takes precedence over artistic order and conventions. In that diocese there are a great many massive tabernacles of particular historical and artistic value and Doctor Grau petitioned Rome for permission not to cover them with the traditional canopy, but that permission was denied.

His artistic sense allowed him to see the parallels between the plastic composition of the sacrifice central to the Mass and Greek tragedy. "In the Mass, there is a dialogue between the celebrant and the choir, between the priest and the faithful, postures and movements are precise and correct, the entreaties and blessings and the sermons pronounced by Bishops seated in faldstools are of the greatest plastic grandeur and the Passion recitations, with their restrained drama, are of exceptional beauty."

Gaudí emphasised how well-chosen the liturgical colours were. "The colours used in the Roman liturgy are not only linked to their meaning, but they are also clear and unmistakable, and the best suited for being easily distinguished at a distance: white, green, red, purple and black. This is not so, however, with the blue and pink that were added later." He had studied liturgical vestments and returned to the simplicity of basilicas, with a beautiful sense of modernity. He was particularly interested in a chasuble with catenary lines that he hoped to propose to the Church hierarchy, after having declined the offer of a priest of the Greek Orthodox Church to use it.

As an architect, he objected to the floodlighting of naves and even more strenuously to use of electric candles on the altar. "On the altar, there should only be real wax candles and flowers, and above them, the crown of the lamps of the candelabrum. On the table where the Holy Oils are consecrated there should also be an abundance of flowers. On the major feast days, the church should be adorned with fragrant flowers." In spite of this, he himself made surprisingly ingenious use of electric light, combining alabaster polyhedra with a myriad of tiny light bulbs and gilded metal. He did not agree with the idea that dim light favours devotion. "The light has to be sufficient, neither too strong nor too dim, since both extremes impede vision. There has to be enough light to be able follow the ceremony with the missal and participate actively in the sacrifice."

In keeping with this attitude, he rejected orchestral masses, with professional choirs and soloists, whose operatic composition converts the faithful into mere spectators. Nor did he accept Kappelmeister Vilanova's *Missa Pastoril*, popular because of its picturesque Christmas flavour, for Midnight Mass, feeling that it was not fitting to the solemn sacrifice. Gaudí's enthusiasm for the Vatican's measures to encourage a return to Gregorian chant was boundless. "If the people do not sing patriotic anthems, they will sing revolutionary ones, and if they do not sing religious songs, they will sing blasphemous or bawdy ones. The people must participate, then, in the Church's songs." He also wished that, during processions, not only the participants but also the spectators should sing liturgical hymns and popular songs. One day, as we were following the Corpus Christi procession and it was held up, he said to me: "There shouldn't be pickets and military cordons, but instead choirs and choral societies on every street corner." He once recounted the dialogue between Saint Ambrose, the bishop of Milan, and the Emperor Theodosius the Great when the latter, on entering the basilica and hearing the voices of the people singing, was moved to ask if they were already in heaven, and received the reply that they were not in heaven yet, but they were in its anteroom.

This explains his studies of acoustics and experiments with sounding boards and bells, for the purpose of endowing the Sagrada Familia with a clear and intense sound quality, his plan for a gynaeceum for female singers, fittingly separated from the male voices, and the novel idea of distributing among the twelve bell towers a determined number of different bells, as if it were a gigantic organ, to accompany the canticles sung in the neighbourhood processions and fill the city with sacred music on the major feast days.

His attachment to the spirit of the liturgy led him to refuse to plan and build the church of the Teresan Sisters' convent, because they required that it remain a private church with no access from outside the convent. In explaining the incident, he gave a number of sound reasons for not accepting such an ill-advised project, and finished by adding bitterly: "They have built a church in isolation from the outside world, in an apartment, with iron bars!"

His profound sense of the liturgy, in combination with his acute observation, allowed him to discern which was the true Chapel of the Holy Sacrament in the cathedral of Barcelona before examination of existing documents confirmed his opinion. In the same way, he was able to decipher correctly the symbolism of the unusual high chapel in the apse of the cathedral of Palma de Mallorca, which was later correctly deduced by Doctor Miralles from the Cathedral archives that he was in charge of at the time.

Dr. Juan Bautista Grau y Bellespinós (1832-1893), Bishop of Astorga.

The Lyrical Christian

Once again, his meditation on inexorable death, upon the decease of his mother, and his sense of the precariousness of life, on suffering from Mediterranean fevers, marked the beginning of Gaudí's embrace of asceticism. He increasingly shed the comforts of life and the progressive austerity of his diet and apparel, stemming more from hygienic considerations than pious ones, led, by way of a desire for sacrifice, to heroic achievements. Once he had recovered from his bouts with fever, he began a punishing fast that not even his parents' entreaties or the pleas of his closest friends could moderate.

Gaudí fasting during lent, 1894.
Drawn by Opisso.

He commented: "Mortification of the body is the happiness of the spirit, as Doctor Torras i Bages rightly said, and mortification of the body is to be found in continuous, persistent work. This is one's strongest support in the face of temptation." He wisely learned to better himself through his setbacks. "You don't learn to walk properly until you have fallen with a jolt. Jolts open the door to conviction." And he, who had been so thoroughly convinced of his strength, confessed: "Every fall is the result of believing too much in oneself."

He intensified his prayerful activities. "The only means of correction is punishment. Man is free to do evil, but he must inevitably face the consequences of that evil. God finds it necessary to correct us constantly, he must punish us constantly, and we must pray to him, 'Lord, punish us, but also console us'."

His spiritual vigour grew continually: "Virtue, a necessity for all, is most important for men, as virtue is derived from *vir*, or man, and virility, or strength." However, to keep him from false humility, the Lord left him with the persistent itch of his irascible self-esteem. "By temperament, I am a fighter, I have struggled incessantly and I have been successful in every endeavour but one: dominating my own bad temper." But he did not give up and strove to find ways of humiliating himself in his own eyes: "It is of great use in failure to take the blame on oneself, even if it is not merited, because this serves to let the truth shine through, although just the opposite would seem to be the case. This is a most rewarding effort, since the enemy of good works is self-esteem. It must be dominated and humbled through perseverance even in the absence of any immediate success." His humiliation reached its culmination with the financial crisis that brought work on the Sagrada Familia to a halt, when he decided to beg for charity, with the threefold torment of feeling himself useless, receiving terrible disappointments and tiring himself spiritually and physically for months on end. "I decided to beg for charity, but it was excruciating for me and I did it very badly."

Since his youth he had been generous and in the latter stages of his striving for perfection he became voluntarily poor. He endowed a benefice on the Sanctuary of Our Lady of Mercy at Reus, for his mother's soul, and he spent his money on the works of the Sagrada Familia's schools. He renounced commissions and therefore any material income, and he used his savings to support struggling artists and finally, to support the construction and rites of his church.

He praised the benefits of poverty and its influence on artistic creation: "Poverty should not be confused with wretchedness. Poverty leads to elegance and beauty; riches lead to opulence and complication, and these can never be beautiful."

He came to find pain, and even penury, necessary to counteract the artist's pride: "In order for the artist not to lose his bearings with the exaltation of art, he must undergo pain and abjectness. In order to guard against any lapse of discipline, the scourge is required; it is the only means of not losing one's way."

In his inexorable progress towards this mortification, he exclaimed: "It is good for both the body and soul to suffer the cold in winter and the heat in summer," and "One must eat just enough to stay alive."

The final phase of painful ordeal and total sacrifice to God came with the disappearance of the last vestiges of his family life. After his father's death, he remained alone with his niece Rosa, in his cottage at Güell Park. She was the daughter of his sister Rosa, who had married young and unwisely to an Andalusian musician of a bohemian bent who drank too heavily; she died in childbirth. Rosa, alone at the cottage and missing the company of her old uncle, who would sometimes go out walking with her, prone to tuberculosis and heart problems, began drinking Agua del Carmen, a popular patent remedy containing alcohol, in secret, because it seemed to give her strength, and she finally died of a heart attack. The six years that this tragic situation lasted were a bitter ordeal for Gaudí, who abhorred drunkenness and had combated it among his workmen, but who was unable to free his beloved niece from its grasp.

Gaudí was left alone; when his nephew Josep offered to live with him, he rejected the offer and replied that he would make do by himself at the cottage, or, if not, he would move into his workshop at the Sagrada Familia. When his nephew objected that he might fall ill, Gaudí replied firmly: "That is all planned; I will go to the hospital."

With the death of his friend Maragall and then, shortly afterwards, of his beloved patron, Conde Güell, and his friend Doctor Torras i Bages, Gaudí was plunged into absolute solitude. "My closest friends are dead; I have no family, no clients, no fortune, nothing. Now I can dedicate myself wholly to my church." When I went to invite him to my wedding and he explained his life to us , my fiancée asked him, in surprise, "How can you live so alone?" Gaudí replied:

"I am not alone, I am surrounded by an endless array of marvels." "Then you must be very happy indeed," answered my fiancée. In this world, happiness always belongs to others.

During this time, Gaudí carried out heroic acts of charity. For over a year, he provided a home for the sculptor Mani, who was not at all suitable company, as much because of his character and habits as because of the afflictions to which he was prone. He called on stonecutters who had fallen ill with tuberculosis while working on the Sagrada Familia in contravention of the preventive measures that Gaudí had prescribed but that the workers, out of their lack of understanding and their acquired habits, could not be convinced to observe.

The plasterers' foreman, who intensely admired Gaudí, offered to spend the nights at the cottage in Güell Park to keep him company, leaving his own family at home. Gaudí accepted and after having supper at the church, they would go back the cottage where they each slept in a room on either side of bathroom that they shared. The plasterer had problems with his nose and Gaudí took him to see an eminent skin specialist who was a friend of his. After submitting to a lengthy but unsuccessful treatment, the specialist informed Gaudí that it was an incurable cancer. Gaudí said nothing to the sick man but continued in his company, and he explained to me: "The only difference is that I limit myself to washing at the tap instead of in the bathroom, so that Lorenzo can go on washing himself there and not come to suspect the seriousness of his illness."

Torras i Bages (1846-1916).

In the end, he left the cottage and ensconced himself in his church, where he slept in a small room, filled, as was the rest of the workshop, with plaster moulds, rolls of paper and books. This is when he insisted most on his maxim: "The artist must live like a monk, not like a friar," and when, feeling the onslaught of age he exclaimed, "As I feel my body growing weaker, I feel my spirit growing more agile."

He continued to work uninterruptedly, because he felt that time was slipping away from him faster and faster. His slogan was the initial Hippocratic aphorism: *ars longa, agita brevis*. In keeping with his own imposing motto "One must become better unceasingly" he gathered up a store of magnificent discoveries, creating beauty on beauty, perfection on perfection. His life was now absolutely ascetic, his piety bordering on mysticism, and the works of his last ten years rose beyond the limits of the highest achievements of architecture, carried upward on a growing lyrical exaltation. He was pleased with the polychrome finish on the first bell tower and he showed it to, saying to me: "Just look at that finial! Doesn't it seem to join the Earth to Heaven? This shining mosaic is the first thing that sailors will see when they arrive in Barcelona. What a radiant welcome!" He was just as satisfied with the final model for the naves of the church, but he was still frustrated that he could not build them to the full extension, and he took as his own Da Vinci's lamentation: "What beautiful things I could make, if only I had the means!"

Purified in the crucible of pain and loosed from all of his earthly ties, he dedicated himself entirely to the service of God, to the ardent task of glorifying Him. In this way he was worthy of the divine gift that he been endowed with and he became the architect of the Lord.

In his fulfilment, he found the sensation of becoming a child again, as prescribed in the Gospel. He recalled his feelings as a boy on hearing the office in praise of the Virgin and he showed that tender filial devotion to Mary that is the sign of glorious predestination. One night, he came over to me and said, "I am going to the Basilica de La Merced, to say a few things to the Virgin." Although his edifying conduct and his selfless work were in themselves true and profound prayer, he regretted that he could not feel a permanent union with God: "Only the angels are capable of constant prayer. We humans are incapable of it."

He, who was in the habit of sagely advising his aged father to be careful, particularly when crossing the street, was struck by a tram late in the afternoon of June 7 1926, when he was on his way, as was his custom, to the San Felipe Neri oratory for vespers, withdrawn into his spirit and oblivious to everything around him. He was taken, providentially, to the old Santa Cruz hospital, as he had wished, and he died three days later, at mid-afternoon, his last words being "Amen", in response to a priest's prayer, and "My God!"

Gaudí in hospital, June 11th, 1926.
Drawing by Lorenzo Brunet.
Mediterráneo, Barcelona,
2nd April 1927.

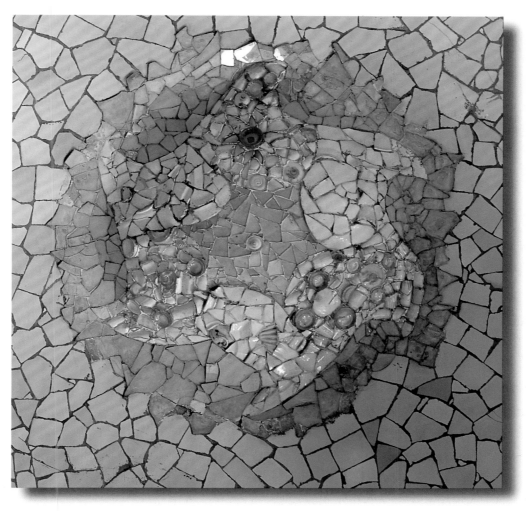

GAUDÍ'S WORKS

IN THE LIFE AND WORKS OF GAUDÍ, TAKEN AS A WHOLE, WE CAN SEE a providential chain of events that allowed this great artist to use his exceptional gifts to produce works that are as exquisite as they are numerous and varied, in spite of the inability of many of his contemporaries to appreciate them. The starting point of his productive career was his encounter with a refined and generous patron, Eusebi Güell i Bacigalupi, who showed himself to be a Maecenas worthy of our genius's art.

Whereas in the other arts an artist can find expression for his creative spirit even if he does not possess the material means, in architecture the work must be built and the dream must be made palpable reality in order for the artist's creation to exist. Güell discovered Gaudí through a modest piece, a showcase that the Comella glove shop had sent to the Paris Exposition in 1878. This expressive, delicate work in glass, wood and metal captivated his gentleman's spirit to such a degree that he arranged to meet the young architect and introduced him to Barcelona's high society, showing extraordinary confidence in him.

The gentleman and the artist understood and influenced each other, particularly during Güell's last years, when his intimate personal life took on a truly Franciscan style. Gaudí described his exceptional client, saying: "He is a true gentleman; he has a princely character, reminiscent of the Medicis of Florence and the Dorias of Genoa." And he pointed out that the mother of "Don Eusebio", as Gaudí called him, was from a noble Genoese family.

He had a genuinely aristocratic spirit and he felt a great deal of social and civic responsibility, and as he also possessed a refined sensibility, the arts held an irresistible attraction for this man of affairs. Güell was thrifty to the extent that he would cut off the unused portion of a piece of writing paper, but he was generous to a fault when it came to works of art or beneficence.

This exemplary patrician's great merits earned him the title of Conde de Güell. The newly named Count commissioned Gaudí to create his coat of arms, and in in doing so, he ignored traditional heraldic canons and produced a unique and very intentional composition. The lower edge, instead of being semicircular, is a catenary curve (the same as seen in the doors of the Palau Güell, chosen by the Count over other more orthodox shapes also proposed by Gaudí). The shield is divided into two fields azur by the outline of the mansion's cupola, with its pinnacle. To the left, under the motto "Hoy señor" (Today a lord), there is an owl perched on a quarter moon, symbolising prudence and wisdom in adversity; to the right, under the second part of the motto, "Ayer pastor" (Yesterday a shepherd), there is a flying dove carrying a cogwheel, an illusion to the industrial endeavour at the Colonia Güell in Santa Coloma de Cervelló. Above the shield are the knightly attributes, a visored helmet, gorget and breastplate, and over the helmet, the count's coronet, with a dove, symbol of the spirit, crowning the composition.

The eminent industrialist that organised and directed the Colonia Güell said: "I fill the Count's pockets and Gaudí empties them." While his mansion was being built on the Calle Nueva de la Rambla, the Count was away for some time and when he returned and went to see how the work was progressing, his secretary, horrified at the cost being run up on the project, tried to soften the blow before giving him the figures. When at last he did, the Count replied: "Is that all?"

It is a shame that there is no record of the conversations between patron and artist, particularly at Güell Park, over the many years that both of them lived in that admirable development.

Other enlightened spirits followed Conde Güell's example and promoted Gaudí's rich production in the field of secular architecture. At the same time, Martorell's admiration for Gaudí and his friendship with eminent clergymen made his efforts in religious architecture possible.

Gaudí's works are exceptionally diverse, although his mechanical concepts and plasticity are the same throughout, bearing the immediately identifiable stamp of his artistic personality, a blend of traditional, original, baroque and technical aspects. We have seen all of this for ourselves on our visits to his works, with Gaudí himself providing us that access. It is truly satisfying to state that, without exception, he was pleased to show us all of them, both his work in Catalonia and that in Castile. After most of these visits, Gaudí would give us further explanations and details, as noted below with each of the individual works.

Eusebio Güell (1846-1918).

INNOVATIVE DEVELOPMENT

Some see Gaudí as revolutionary. Nothing could be further from the truth. He was of the opinion that the outcome of revolutionary attitudes and action, in any context whatsoever, is always negative.

He thought that progress was possible only through reference to the past and with the support of the advances made by our predecessors. "We must base our work on the past in order to create anything of value, but at the same time avoid repeating past errors." His originality consisted of reviving the most timeworn fundamental concepts. "True originality is always a matter of returning to the source." He rightly believed that "there is no need to try to be original, because each artist's style – a word that comes from *stylus* – is already within them and will manifest itself spontaneously".

Revision of Historical Styles

Gaudí began his career at a time when everyone still looked to the past. The master builders were still using the then outmoded neo-classical formulae and the leading architects were restoring medieval buildings following the stylish dictates of Romanticism derived from Ruskin's ideas, which pervaded not only literature but also art and criticism, and then adapting their own projects and new building programmes to them. At first, Gaudí worked along the same lines as his colleagues and he also turned his attention to the past, although not as an end in itself, but rather as a starting point to build on the legacy of previous generations. "Science is learned on the basis of principles and art is learned on the basis of past works." Thus, rather than rummaging in catalogues of mummified forms that were held up as representative of medieval styles and replacing treatises in the style of Vignola with the ideas of theorists such as Viollet, the young architect undertook his own revision of the plastic and aesthetic aspects of architectural styles. He pointed out their faults, structural in ancient works and artistic in the Gothic era, while at the same time extracting the sense of composition and modulation peculiar to each one, allowing him to evolve them in a modern idiom (but not in the Modern Style) and to use them freely and with his own personal touch.

Architects soon gravitated into two groups. One of these groups practised a submissive medievalism, those individuals with a fine archaeological sense succeeding and the rest becoming mired in a thoroughly deplorable pastiche of Gothic, Romanesque and even Byzantine Romanesque (!). The other group, dissidents, popularised Egyptian, classical and Etruscan (!) forms, totally divorced from any meaning, as a means of deliverance. All of them came to assign, grotesquely, one of the historical styles to each type of building and to concoct horrible combinations of forms from different styles, with truly deplorable results. Gaudí, delving deeply into the artistic spirit of the past's greatest achievements, made the capital discovery of modulation as a characteristic aspect not only of each style but also of each artist, relegating attention to formal details to a secondary position. This allowed him to create vital works when using a specific style and to create a new style when applying the principles of modulation in an original manner, enveloped in natural forms. Gaudí's dazzling results inspired a number of architects who were tired of doing nothing but copying the past and rushed with abandon into aberrations of the Modern Style. They were working from the assumption that not only did the Modern Style not require any sort of reference to historical works, but that it should even go so far as to contradict them. In the place of rational (plastic, constructive, mechanical) architectural elements, they used arbitrary curved forms adorned with blandly sculpted decoration and often in outlandish colours, all of it entwined in plant motifs that, for all their attempts at naturalism, gave a totally artificial result.

Coat of arms of the Honourable Count of Güell.
Painted by Mirabent on parchment following an idea and sketch by Gaudí, ignoring the usual, stereotyped rules of heraldry. The lower part of the shield is enclosed within a catenary, as Güell had used arches of this form for the gates to his palace. The composition is centred around the palace's spire; an owl above the 3rd quarter of the moon can be seen to one side – symbol of prudence in adversity – while on the other is a dove carrying a cogwheel, expressing industry. Above the birds is the inscription "Today a lord, yesterday a shepherd", nicely summing up worldly honours. The breastplate, gorget and the helmet, with a count's coronet and a dove, expressing energy in the service of spirituality, top the coat of arms.

A project done by Gaudí while a student, from the courtyard of the Barcelona Provincial Council (October 6th, 1876).

Tradition and Innovation

In contrast to the archaeological traditionalism of some architects and the arbitrary improvisation of others, Gaudí showed a living and soundly reasoned traditionalism. This allowed him to carry out his marvellous restoration of the cathedral of Palma de Mallorca, where it is difficult to distinguish the authentic Gothic elements from the modern additions completing them or to discern which plateresque and baroque elements he transformed, finishing them in such a way that is only barely discernible. It allowed him to build the archaic Doric colonnade in Güell Park "just as the Greeks would have done in one of their Mediterranean colonies". It allowed him to build the medieval mansion of Bellesguard, a building as thoroughly Gothic as it is modern, the block of apartments on Calle Caspe, in such total harmony with Catalan Baroque, the Conde Güell's freely interpreted Venetian mansion, the Mudejar house on Calle de las Carolinas, the Moorish pavilions at the Exposition and the early Gothic of the Sagrada Familia, strengthened and improved upon, to be seen in the bright Mediterranean light.

The Doric, Gothic and Baroque in his work are profoundly genuine, but they are his Doric, his Gothic and his Baroque, unique, inimitable and personal.

Gaudíism

With the regular swings characteristic of the History of Art, it was only natural that the sober neo-classical execution should lead to a baroque reaction. Furthermore, Baroque was the last style to really take root in this country and in our soul, and the only living tie to the past, since both Neo-classicism and Romanticism were reheated dishes offering no sustenance. We can understand, then, Gaudí's preference for these dynamic forms and how, working from a baroque starting point with his slow and steady progression, verified in physical studies, he arrived at vitalistic forms, at the cosmic plasticity of Güell Park, the Casa Battló and the Casa Milà, where for the first time architecture overflowed the limits of its field and burst in on the field of the representative arts.

When geometrical uniformity and conversion into canon began to restrict this flowering of naturalism, he created his masterpiece, the Gaudí order in the final plan for the naves of the Sagrada Familia, representing the application of a baroque sensibility to modern architecture, an architecture grown weary of the diagrammatic approach popularised by Le Corbusier, a sort of architectural Cubism that is more a product of the technical possibilities offered by new materials rather than of any true artistic sensibility.

We see, then, that Gaudíism is not the result of a presumptuous personal insistence on originality, but rather the fruit of an ongoing evolution, beginning with the initial formulation of the architectural problem and following with the selection of successive historical solutions to that problem on the basis of the most objective and stringent critical judgement, leading to new forms and results that never ceased in their advance and refinement, right up to the end of the master's laborious life.

CHARACTERISTIC PERIODS

The various different periods of Gaudí's production cannot be clearly differentiated, because the time involved in constructing a work of architecture often gives rise to a situation where a project with a new approach is begun while other previous projects with a different orientation are still being carried out. We can speak, for example, of groups of related works on the basis of plastic types and mechanical and constructive solutions that point to characteristic landmarks in the always ascending course of Gaudí's creation. The following are the major works in each group.

Early Period

This period comprises Gaudí's production while working as assistant to other architects and minor works on a personal scale, dating from the final years of his studies and the first few years afterwards. In the former case, he worked on projects that were already drawn up and he focused his imagination on the details, bringing to bear on them a delightfully assertive use of advanced geometric forms and a preference for structural elements with clear mechanical functions.

Chapel in the Church of the Montserrat Monastery (1875-1877). Project by the architect Villar, where the banked arches, the movement of the reliefs, the inclined pedestals and the parabolic tori at the bases of the columns were contributed by Gaudí.

Works in the Parque de la Ciudadela (1877-1882). The master builder Fontserè employed Gaudí as his assistant when he planned and built the Cascade (modelled on a fountain in the Parc de Longchamp in Marseilles), the railings of the Placita Aribau and the park's railings and gates. Fontserè had a rather poor neo-classical style and he was soon outstripped by his assistant, mostly as a result of the fluency with which he handled the classical elements, as seen in the lintel of the door to the aquarium and especially in the echinus mouldings, the acroteria, with their clearly hyperboloid volumes, the lively palmettes of floral elements – enriched by a generosity of planes – and the dynamically naturalistic fauna used in the decorations, fine examples of which can be seen in the circular panels decorating the façade of the aquarium and in the pilasters of the Placita Aribau, where a sharp profile emphasises stability.

Furniture and liturgical pieces. Gaudí made concise plans in his diary for a desk for himself, which he later designed with painstaking attention to detail, with a cylindrical cover, drawers in the middle and suspended cabinets on the sides. Instead of the eight legs usually found on this type of bureau, Gaudí designed it with only four very light, delicately turned legs with gussets, joined simply half-way up by crosspieces. The cabinetmaker was somewhat dismayed by the absence of upper crosspieces and told the architect that the desk would not be stable. Gaudí explained to me: "He just could not understand the function of the gussets and I finally gave him the example of a donkey that, when it is loaded with its panniers, is more stable." The cabinetmaker complained: "Gaudí always makes things too complicated. If you commission him to build a washbowl, he makes a basket for you instead." One of Conde Güell's relatives replied: "Yes, but it holds water."

The showcase, mentioned earlier, that the Comella shop sent to the Paris Exposition had a woodwork base, with its corners reinforced with decorative supports, supporting the elegant metal and glass main body, providing perfect visibility, crowned by an ingenious structure projecting in various directions. This, his first work, shows his taste for combining different materials.

For the oratory of the Palacio de Comillas (Santander, 1878), he made a seat of honour with arms, high back and kneeler, and pews whose opulent decoration contrasts with the lightness of the uprights in the form of miniature columns and with the plastic richness of the carved elements of these furnishings, causing the surprising impression mentioned earlier.

For the chapel of the Jesus and Mary School in San Andrés del Palomar (1879-1881), he made the altar, the monstrance, the lighting fixtures and mosaic decoration of apse. These works showed the same decorative and ornamental characteristics as the others mentioned here.

Lamp standards at Plaza Real and Barceloneta. These lamp standards for public lighting are still the most beautiful in Barcelona. In spite of their extreme restraint, they have not aged. Once again we see Gaudí's combination of different materials, in this case stone and metal. The stone base, with its sloping faces, provides stability and connects to the underlying flagstones. The lamp standard itself is wrought iron, never a particularly attractive material, with graceful individual buttressing of the two arms supporting the glass globe.

The last three works mentioned above belong chronologically to the following group, but in view of their minor importance, we have included them with the other similar works of his initial period.

An engraving published in *I.C.* (September 20th, 1880), stated to be the work of Gaudí. Drawn by Castelucho.

Mudejar-moorish

The works in this group, built outside Barcelona, are characterised by horizontal bands on the first floors and, on the top floor, the harmoniously rhythmic pilaster strips topped in mitred arches, and by the use of brick corbels. Gaudí considered the Arabs to possess a superior mechanical sense: "The Arabs' corbels are closer to funicular forms than the medieval arches of the Christians."

Decoration is eminently polychrome. Obtained basically through the contrast between brickwork and masonry, it is completed with profuse ceramic finishes and, on finials, with Moorish-inspired cupolas also faced with coloured ceramics.

These works are constructed basically of brick, using curious techniques to avoid having to break the bricks to size, alternating flat courses with upright ones and with windowsills using both the width and length of the bricks.

There is a remarkable resemblance between some of these brickwork elements and those used by the architect Martorell in the Salesian Sisters' convent, a project on which he was assisted by Gaudí and Martorell's most interesting work. The two architects influenced each other and this collaboration and influence led to Martorell's very high opinion of his assistant.

Towards the end of this period, the greater prestige and more central location of Gaudí's projects led him to begin using worked stone, modifying his compositions accordingly with the use of elements derived from the Gothic, marking the transition to the following period.

Casa Vicens (1883-1885). Located in the neighbourhood of Gracia, at Calle de las Carolinas 24/26. This is a spacious house with a garden on the south side, containing the traditional fountain and a corner pavilion. It is a delectable work, with the play of projecting bodies on corbeled beams, hanging guttae, a delicate use of carpentry with turned pieces in window grilles and ingeniously incorporated into the construction of the interior. A curious touch is found in the double doors with narrow leaves that open simultaneously using a double rack concealed in the lintel.

For the fountain, he made adventurous use, for the first time, of a paraboloid vault. The decoration shows the architect's incipient lyrical naturalism. "When I went to take measurements, the whole plot was covered in small yellow flowers and I took these for the ornamental pattern of the ceramic work." Gaudí also encountered a bushy palmetto palm, whose fans, reproduced in wrought iron, fill the frame of grate and the door into the house. In the interior, aside from the suspended vault of the smoking room, with its struts and stalactites, and the coffered ceiling in the salon, the roofs have wooden beams on corbels and the small vaults between them are decorated with bright green leaves studded with brilliant red cherries. From the dining room's whimsical ceiling hang several birds on almost invisible threads and on the ample reveals between the dining room and the gallery, Gaudí had flocks of birds on the wing painted. In front of the gallery, he placed a fountain with a metal mesh screen; the water is turned into fine spray that sparkles with magic iridescence in the sun.

Güell Estate Hunting Lodge (1882). It was planned to be located on the coast at Garraf. Gaudí drew up a plan along the same aesthetic lines as the Casa Vicens, but with more picturesque shape in fitting with the setting. It has a stepped form, beginning with a portico, followed by a rotunda and finishing in a robust tower. It was never built.

Villa Quijano (1883-1885). A small country house, also known as *El Capricho*, on the outskirts of Comillas (Santander). It is similar in composition to the preceding work, but it is set on a foundation of ashlars the full height of the basement. In the cornice, he replaced the pilaster strip with corbels of Gothic proportions, interrupted by the louvers emerging from the prominent roof. Above the portico, there is a slender cylindrical watchtower topped by a winged roof on slender metal supports. When Gaudí showed me his numerous drawings for the project, he said: "The owner's name is Díaz de Quijano, and I said to myself, Quijano, Quijada ... Quixote, and thought that it would be better not to go, because perhaps we might not get along." And it was built without Gaudí ever seeing it. For the

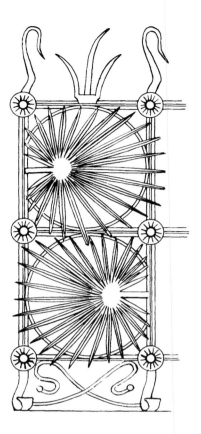

Railing using palmetto leaves (Casa Vicens, Barcelona). A fine example of wrought-iron and foundry work, commemorating a palmetto that had to be uprooted during construction.

ridge of the roof, he had planned a graceful and decorative crest incorporating the name of the property and its owner, but it was never built.

When he showed me the static calculation of the vaults and columns of the entrance portico, he told me that it had occurred to him to slant the columns to reduce their bulk.

Casa Güell pavilions and gate (1884). On this property located between Les Corts and Pedralbes, now divided by subsequent urban development, Gaudí built enclosing walls and the entrance gate and pavilions. Here too he used horizontal bands, crowning them with a brick and ceramic cornice. The walls and pavilions sit on stone foundations supporting structures of brick and rubble. "Since they were low buildings, I decided to use rubble for them, since it is the most inexpensive and the best insulator. We brought in some craftsmen from Sucs to do this work." Instead of pointed arches, he used parabolic shapes of brick corbeling, without a keystone in narrow windows and doors and with rowlocks in the wider ones. Instead of accentuating angles with protruding brick, they form graceful hollows, where the downpipes were situated.

The main wall is pierced by the famous gate with its chained dragon, with the porter's lodge to the left and the stables to the right. The vestibules of these buildings are on a square plan which becomes an octagon by means of pendentives from the corners and are covered by a vault pierced in the centre to finish in a small louver. Worth noting here is the absence of any angle where these two elements meet, the join instead taking a definitely hyperboloid form.

All of the decoration is eminently rational. It is made up of brick frames, the brick courses tying the rubble and the facing of smooth and relief-ornamented moulded cement pieces. These facings were used to protect the rubble from the rain instead of rendering, which does not adhere well to earth. A curious polychrome effect is achieved by alternating courses of yellow and red brick and enriched by the small pieces of glazed material encrusted in the mortar. The use of colour in finials and cupolas increased with ever more continuous ceramic facing.

The grilles of the side doors contain elements forged in three dimensions, but this concept of volume reaches its maximum expression in the dragon gate, a masterpiece of ironwork, where the metal is used in all of its forms. The structure is made of commercial T and L bars, which lose their industrial appearance in the grooves of the wing. The rectangular base is formed by a diagonal grid holding cast-iron plaques with a rosette adorning each one. Above this is the dragon, full-bodied, anatomically constructed on the basis of the skeleton. The spine is made from a cast-iron piece around which is coiled a round iron spiral, thicker near the head and where it forms the body and more slender in the neck and in the sinuous curves of the tail. The changes of plane are constant, particularly on arriving at the head, which is seen from the front with its menacing mouth agape brandishing rows of pointed teeth. The legs and feet are articulated from the body and covered in pointed scales made of embossed sheet iron and the toes end in nails. The left front leg is mounted on a rotary joint and connected to chain that tenses and moves it when the gate is opened. The wings curve in nervous, undulating folds to carry the wingtips to the lock of the gate, binding the whole of the dragon's body; the wings are made of iron mesh, giving them a transparency reminiscent of insect wings. The imposing glare, the numerous spines bristling all over the body and the movement of the tail all add to the impression of hostility.

Among other lesser works, some of which have disappeared completely, worth mentioning as an example of ultra-economical industrial construction are the factory, installations, offices and workers' living quarters of the *Obrera Mataronense* (1878-1882) in Mataró, a complex that was never completed.

The machine room was covered by a flat tile roof supported by parabolic arches of laminated timber, which allowed him to turn the side walls into curtain walls.

Shortly afterwards (1883), Gaudí took charge of the construction of the Sagrada Familia. He had attended the ceremony of laying the first stone as one of the assistants to the architect Villar, who only managed to build the walls and buttresses of the crypt up to half their height.

Arab pavilions (1887-1888). Commissioned by the Compañía Transatlántica, Gaudí planned and built two pavilions in Arab-Andalusian style –very much in fashion at the time, one for the Maritime Exposition in Cadiz and the other for the Universal Exposition in Barcelona. We

Top of the railing (Casa Güell). Railings are usually designed as a plane surface. However, Gaudí worked in three dimensions, giving them depth, decorating their tops with crowns between the curved uprights.

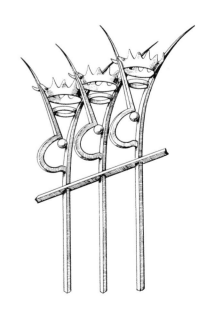

have already mentioned that his use of contrasting curved forms, in stalactites and elements framing the tilework, caused a sensation with the public and the critics.

Palau Güell (1886-1889). Situated in the Calle Nueva de la Rambla at numbers 3 and 5. This work, carried out at the same time as the last works mentioned above, represents the stately culmination of the type of composition included in this group and, at the same time, on the basis of the confident use of elements with a Gothic cast, marks the transition to the following period.

The work has a deliberate majesty. Gaudí commented that Conde Güell's second surname was Italian and he happily repeated, "Don Eusebio was a *Dux*, in his talent, his good taste and his spiritual refinement."

Gaudí used Garraf marble profusely here, not only for the façade but also for the austere jambs and lintels of the interior doors, the magnificent elements between roof beams and the beautiful colonnades leading to the galleries. The columns have hyperbolic capitals and support parabolic arches, rather than properly pointed Gothic arches. The various alternative projects drawn up for the façade show doorways with lintels, or with flattened arches, or with catenary arches, and the latter were finally chosen. Gaudí continued working with a medievalist composition, using series of narrow openings and projecting volumes on corbels, whose strong and robust diagrammatic profile is repeated under the two-storey lateral galleries, but are more finely drawn and finish in curves under the central, one-storey gallery. The lintels in this central body alternate between high and low and those of the lateral galleries are all at the same tall height. The architect continued to dispense with cornices and there are only the austere dripstones and hood moulds, the highest of which, flanked by short balustrades, form three stepped gable ends, crowned by the conical caps of the ventilation shafts.

The façade has no sculpture or polychrome but is sumptuously decorated with varied ironwork elements. Over all is the monumental shield of Catalonia, situated between the two doorways and fixed to the stone by undulating ribbons attached with unique forged spikes; the shield is not flat, but conical, and is topped by chain-link helmet on which an aggressive-looking eagle is perched. The sober, robust ironwork doors are as austere as the façade, but not so the uprights, which are worked with the Güell coats of arms, perhaps in an overly baroque fashion, against a background of railings that are exaggeratedly twisting and lumpy.

The mansion has six floors. In the basement are the stables, the stableboy's quarters and the tack room; access is by means of a gently sloping ramp for horses and a steeper helicoidal one for the servants. The ventilation shafts and an open court make it a salubrious place for horses. On the ground floor are the large vestibule, with the main stairway in the centre, the service stairway to one side and the porter's apartment on the other. At the back is the coach house and the doorways giving access to the ramps leading to the basement. Between the ground floor and the main floor is a partial mezzanine housing the library, the archives and household administration offices.

The main floor is laid out around a hall which rises through the two upper floors and emerges onto the roof in the elongated curves of the cupola, held up by four large corner pendentives, with four parabolic arches and a double roof. These arches lead into flourishes of vaulting that end in the louvers of the monumental space. The main stairway leads to a large vestibule; the central room leads from the hall to the reception room, next to which there is a dressing room with accompanying toilets; the hall has a chapel, with the organ console to one side and a small sacristy to the other. The hall is also connected to the dining room and the latter to a small sitting room and the billiard room. On the other side of the dining room is a small dumbwaiter connected to the kitchen, on the top floor.

Above the main floor is a sitting room reached by the hall stairway, a study, seven large bedrooms with their individual toilets, a large bathroom and the servants' quarters. And on the top floor are the kitchen, the laundry and eleven servants' rooms, along with the organ's pipes, giving its sound a velvety quality. On the roof are the cupola covering the hall, in the centre, with four lanterns, surrounded by eighteen curious conical chimneys, covered in polychrome ceramics, forming a surprising and picturesque ensemble.

Woodwork elements are curiously resolved, particularly on the main floor, where the windows piercing the façade are held in delicate iron frames and when the wooden shutters

Marble columns (Palau Güell, Barcelona). Using paraboloid arches instead of pointed ones obliged Gaudí to design suitable capitals; he chose a horned or hyperbolical shape for the purpose, associating it with the arches without interruption.

are opened, they fit into the jambs, becoming richly decorative mural elements. The door to the salon, decorated on both faces with sculpted panels and the door to the oratory, inlaid with shell and decorated with painted copper panels, are of great splendour. But where wood-work reaches its maximum expression is in the coffered ceilings. The one running above the stairway, with a Gothic concept expressed in a very modern manner, has its main pieces and dividers placed on their arrises and the coffers are broken up into small stepped pyramids ex-tending to the junctions of the main pieces, adorned with handsome ironwork crests. The pro-portions and the moulding of the pyramids gives a striking sensation of depth. In contrast, the coffered ceiling in the reception room is lightest and most original and graceful: the main pieces stand out from the coffers, which are thus seen through an open grid, joined to the roof by turned pieces and small gilded iron struts, creating artistically transmuted grille forms. At the crosspoints of the grid and in the middle of each side, star-shaped crests with turned pen-dants complete this ceiling's majestic air. In the dining room, the open woodwork with pro-jecting elements and mitred forms are a reminder of the Mudejar lines characteristic of Gaudí's earliest works.

Evolved Gothic

When Gaudí took charge of the project for the Sagrada Familia, he not only undertook a crit-ical study of Villar's project, which the Building Committee had never liked, but he also delved even further into the Gothic style, in which the original plan was drawn up.

For the purposes of graphic comparisons, he used Dehio-Bezhold's celebrated compi-lation, but he always had a preference for direct study of the works. We have seen how, in his travels, he had come into contact with the Gothic of the Roussillon, the Catalan Gothic of the Principality and the Mallorcan Gothic, and he studied them carefully. His visit to León showed him the French finery of the *Pulchra Leonina*, and he even travelled to Burgos to vis-it its famed cathedral. His presence there was noticed and when he attended a meeting of in-tellectuals in the social club there, he was bombarded with questions. "I answered evasively, but seeing that they insisted on having me praise that Gothic ostentation, I replied that I found it Manuelino, and they got very angry." When he was recovering from Malta fever in Puigcerdà, he travelled to Toulouse to study the medieval restorations that Viollet had made in Saint Sernin and Notre Dame de Taur. He was disappointed with the unimpressive artistic quality of the work done by the brilliant theorist. "We can go back now," he said, "there is nothing for us to learn from this."

In the end, he came to the conclusion that Gothic is a true style but that it never reached maturity. "Gothic art is imperfect, unfinished. It is the style of the compass and the formula, of industrial repetition. Its stability is based on the permanent shoring of the buttresses; it is a de-fective body held up on crutches. It has no overall unity. The structure is not connected to the geometrised decoration that adorns it; the decoration is false and could be eliminated without marring the work in the slightest. The proof that Gothic works are deficient in their plasticity is that they are most moving when they are mutilated, covered in ivy and lit by moonlight."

He started off by combating the excessive fragmentation of Gothic moulding, and thus on the edges of the vaults of the Sagrada Familia's crypt (1884-1891), he joined the nerves di-rectly to the scotia moulding, eliminating profiles and even intersecting edges. He also elimi-nated capitals and sills from the windows and never used cresting, excessive fretwork or stran-gled sprays, as inappropriate for stone. Lastly, he imbued his work with the classical concept of corporeality and reduced the exaggerated predominance of spaces over masses that robs Gothic structure of potency.

The Episcopal Palace, in Astorga (1887-1893). This work in a Gothic style contrasts sharply with the city's own architectural repertoire, which is more Renaissance. Gaudí was commis-sioned to build it by Bishop Grau, to replace the earlier one that had been destroyed by fire. It is a monumental building, conceived to be fitting for a prelate. It takes the shape of a rec-tangular body, flanked by cylindrical turrets on the corners, and between them on the face of

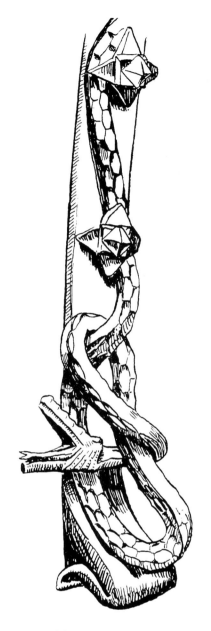

Bottom of the wrought-iron frame of the gate (palau Güell, Barcelona). In a typically Gothic spirit, it ends in a dog's head: however, the twist frees it of medieval rigidity and smoothness, adding a Modernist touch.

Entry to the apartment block (Casa de los Botines, León). This is basically a medieval doorway, but without the canopy, archivolts nor imposts of the Gothic. The obvious quartering of the ashlars, the wall's marked embrasure or bias, in combination with the arch's lobules make up for the lack of ornamentation, demonstrating the artistic value of this feature.

the building, a central body with the throne room. There is an even more prominent projection formed by the chapel and its apses with three subsidiary apses, and on the sides, less prominent rectangular projections, forming an angle. In contrast, on the front and back they are connected by accommodating prisms. All of the rooms are grouped around a central hall, lit from above by a lively array of triangular louvers.

Gaudí's plans show these louvers with Mudejar forms, like those of the capitals in the chapel, which are topped with stalactite decorations. The persistence of the Mudejar concept is also seen in most of the windows, which he built with corbeled stones and without true arches.

As an exception, he did not use parabolic arches for the roof vaults and it is reasonable to suggest that this omission is due to the vicissitudes undergone by the project before receiving the approval of the Real Academia de San Fernando and ultimately of the Ministry of Justice, a formality required by its nature as a public and artistic building. Nevertheless, the arches are highly elongated, in contrast with the relatively low height of their slender supporting columns. This gives the work a unique appearance and at the same time provided the construction with substantial mechanical advantages.

In spite of the many changes of plane on the façade, the continuity of the composition is not lost, as the corners are substituted with cylindrical turrets. The composition based on vertical volumes gives a sensation of lightness and elegance, but the uniform working of the stone and the lack of any accentuation of the width of the openings creates a certain monotony.

Upon Bishop Grau's death, there was a wave of hostility directed at Gaudí, who had brought with him from Barcelona two foremen, masons and carpenters, which had angered the local industrialists. At their instigation, the Cathedral Chapter promptly dismissed Gaudí and his assistants. "We have to get rid of the Catalans – they told us –, and before we left I told them that they would be incapable of finishing the work off properly." Indeed, a "gentlemen who was well-versed in plans – decided to change the layout and when he ordered a wall to be knocked down, several vaults collapsed. Work on the project came to a halt for two years and when it was begun again, they did not know how to build the planned central roof and they made the hall with no source of natural light. During the construction, Gaudí was criticised for working with two foremen instead of one, and he defended himself, saying: "I am like the impresario who had two tenors in his company, and when he was asked why, he replied, 'So that the other one can sing'".

While the Episcopal Palace was being built, Gaudí constructed his first model for the structure of the Sagrada Familia, using extraordinarily elongated ogival arches, pierced spandrels and vertical columns, like those used in Astorga, but he soon replaced the pointed arches with parabolic ones.

He then built the apsidal façade of the Sagrada Familia while at the same time working on the Casa de los Botines in León, which we will discuss below. In both works, the contrast between the different forms of stonework and the emphasis on the thickness of the walls in jambs and on the parapets of openings imbue Gaudí's Gothic with a sense of austerity.

Casa Fernández Andrés (1892-1894). Known popularly as the Casa de los Botines, after the second surname of the Catalan textile wholesaler who was the forebear of the owners who commissioned the work. It occupies a sizeable portion of one side of the Plaza de San Marcelo, in León. Although its ground floor and basement housed its owners' business premises and there were various individual apartments rented out on the upper floors, the whole construction together makes a stately, free-standing mass which, with its corner turrets and the moat separating it from the sidewalk, has all the air of a feudal castle.

As the work had to be stopped for the winter, Gaudí did not begin construction until all of the stone for the façade was ready and all of the structural elements prepared. "The people there were astounded at how fast that great building took shape." "Since it snows heavily there, I covered the building with a roof of very thin slate and the corner turrets with steep spires, deliberately leaving stones projecting from the walls for the snow to build up. After the first snowfall, there was a constant parade of people who came to see this spectacle."

The composition is quite the opposite of the Episcopal Palace in Astorga and is based on horizontal bands emphasised by continuous hood moulds covering the protruding stone courses of the two lower floors. These form a sturdy base and contrast with the vertical lines of projecting corner turrets and those of the louvers and chimneys, which form a crowning crest. The handsome doorway was topped by a lobed arch and comprised a magnificent piece of ironwork with the name of the owners on the tympanum. Above the overhang is a sculpture of a standing Saint George killing the dragon with his lance, a particularly well executed piece by the sculptor Matamala.

In spite of its modernity and its secular nature, this architectural work is an extension of the severe medieval tone with which the magnificent cathedral imbues the city. For this reason, the neighbouring emphatically Renaissance buildings with their banal and busy ornamentation, such as the Casa de los Guzmanes, fade into the background. Its refined and steady Gothic air is missed in the deplorable restoration of León's handsome cathedral. The contrast between the rusticated ashlars and the smooth finish of the hood moulds and, in the foreground, the wrought iron railing that circles the building, give a surprising impression of strength, almost roughness.

He clearly shows us the logical path that should have been followed in the completion of the complex project in Astorga, but his successors were oblivious to this.

The popularity of this work with his fellow architects led some of them to construct buildings in Barcelona with Gothic turrets and spires. Gaudí remarked, jokingly, "They are too farsighted. They are already putting steep roofs on their buildings, in preparation for when the climate changes."

Saint Teresa of Jesus School (1889-1894). On Calle Ganduxer, lined with scattered, low buildings with gardens, one angular mass stands out, embellished with sharp gable ends and prominent corner pinnacles. It has a ground floor and three upper floors, emphasised by horizontal bands joining the masonry of the walls; the frames of the openings and the courses of masonry are done in brick as is the whole of the top floor.

Although the sense of the work is completely Gothic, with the substitution of pointed arches by parabolic ones, we can see all of the constructive strategies that Gaudí had used in his Mudejar works: corbeling, rowlocks and decoration of the top levels with multiple pilaster strips and arches, and, in the gallery over the main entrance, mitred arches and fretwork reminiscent of tracery. He also took advantage of the thickness of the walls to make the windows piercing them rectangular with room for the glazing and shutters in the middle. They are parabolic, giving them greater stability. On the top floor, since the mitred arches are very sharp, he replaced the anti-constructive vertex with a decided chamfer. The ones forming openings are taller and of double thickness, and the decorative blind arches are lower and of only single thickness. Above them are the louvers for ventilation. These variations in height are further emphasised by the crests of the gable ends, finishing in ceramic finials in the shape of doctor's caps.

We also find here the decoration of corners using reworked thickness, ingeniously taken advantage of to fit in a helicoidal column and, in front of it, a modified Carmelite coat of arms: Mount Carmel with the star in the centre and crowned by a cross, and, on either side, the Immaculate Heart of Mary and the Transverberated Heart of Saint Teresa. The pinnacles topping these handsome corners carry the four-armed cross that from that moment on became Gaudí's ubiquitous signature. These crosses, the doctor's caps on the gable ends, the elements of the coats of arms, the tau crosses of the railing panels and the ventilation chimneys are all done in brilliant red, shining out over the austere tone of the façade.

The interior layout consists of rows of rooms along the outside and central corridors with heavy corbeling and slender columns of pressed brick supporting parabolic arches that are extremely elongated to give them negligible thrust.

The conception of the work is fundamentally organic. Each pilaster strip on the façade corresponds to a roof beam and a double corbel in the back wall. On this projection rest the brick pillars supporting the parabolic arches and in the centre of the projections of the middle row are the courts letting light through to the ground floor, creating a sort of hall.

The seats in the vestibule, no longer extant, were noteworthy, and the solutions for fitting woodwork and ironwork to the arches without imposts are ingenious.

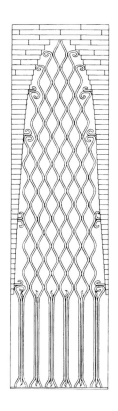

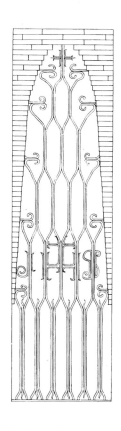

Window-railings
(Saint Teresa of Jesús School, Barcelona). The ground-floor windows are grouped in threes; the name of Jesus can be seen in the hexagonal section of the railings.

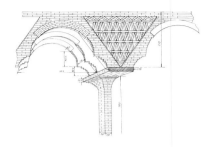

Structure of the roof (Bellesguard mansion, Barcelona). The roof is a marvellous example of the use of brick in construction. The pillars, 1.80 m. apart, expand at the top, to give a cross-section eleven times as great, reinforcing a horizontal plinth, supported by a number of narrow arches on each side, and light open brickwork. The lobulate arches are parabolic in shape and formed of horizontal rows of brick, except at the very top. Above the arches, there is a light roof covered in local slate.

The full project consisted of three wings: two normal wings giving onto Calle Ganduxer (of which Gaudí did the one on the upper side) and one placed crosswise behind them, where the chapel was situated, the treatment of which in the final project (1908-1910) was highly interesting. We have already mentioned how Gaudí refused to build it with the modifications required of him.

When construction of the School was approximately half-finished, he began work on the Façade of the Nativity, in whose architecture we find, in sublimated form, all of the achievements of the preceding work: substantial embrasures, corbels forming double lobes in the arches, very pointed gable ends and helicoidal elements, all of the greatest simplicity and invaded by the most exuberant decoration and ornamentation ever seen, expressive of the naturalist manner that we will discuss below.

Shortly after beginning work on the façade, Gaudí drew up a project for a convent-school for the Franciscan missionaries in Tangier (1892-1902), one that was highly appropriate to its purpose and to the country where it was to be situated. In this project he experimented with circular towers with a parabolic profile, joined by a series of apertures arranged helicoidally, an approach that he later used for the bell towers of the Sagrada Familia, which he had already started building on a square plan.

The day that he showed me these plans, I could not hide my surprise at seeing this precedent to the forms used later in his masterpiece, and Gaudí remarked, referring also to the cupola of the hall in the Palau Güell: "You see, I haven't changed at all. The more I think about these new architectural forms, the more convinced I am that I must use them."

Bellesguard mansion (1900-1902). Although this work is chronologically later than the others in this group and although its plasticity fits in to a great extent with Gaudí's later style, we have placed it here in view of its quintessential Gothic composition. Gaudí chose the most select elements offered by secular Gothic, in homage to King Martín, who had built a villa on the site as a retreat, from which he could see the sea and the galleys as they arrived in port.

The architect maintained and completed the remaining fragments of the royal towers, joining them in a rectangular area forming a mirador. In the entryway, framed by the towers, is the barred coat of arms of Bellesguard, with a shining sun in upper right corner and in the opposite corner, a woman shielding her eyes from the sun with her hand. He moved the road over the Vilana arroyo, supporting it on vaults and robust inclined columns, so that the two towers would remain a part of the property. For the window of the vestibule, he designed a stained glass pane depicting the Magi – of which eventually only the star was made – and the entryway benches are decorated with barred and crowned fish, symbolising Catalonia's maritime hegemony in the Mediterranean.

Located at Calle Bellesguard number 46, it was commissioned by María Sagués, widow of Figueras, an enthusiastic admirer of Gaudí's art.

The walls and the workers' cottage are topped with merlons, to fit in with the restored portion.

The mansion is built on an approximately square plan, with a projection running the whole height of the façade with the doorway and topped by a spire bearing a cross, and another semi-hexagonal projection running half the height of the southern side. This projection is covered by a terrace, while the other two main bodies are topped by truncated pyramids, the larger one housing twin louvers. Their gable ends and the merlons of the pyramids and catwalks – which run all the way round the roof –, along with the chimneys and the spire mentioned earlier, give the building a picturesque and constantly varied silhouette. The attics are lit by a gallery of small windows supported by helicoidal columns and from among them protrude the beaks that serve as gargoyles for draining water from the roof.

Each course of the gallery corresponds to a slim brick arch with joined spandrels, supporting the roof. Thus, the plasticity, the construction, the robust structure and the utilitarian aspects are more accentuated here than at the Teresan Sisters' convent and are combined in a lively synthesis. The brick arches are supported on projecting courses above divided platforms resting on rows of pillars. All of the thrusts of this arched structure are neutralised by means of small struts incorporated into the ironwork.

On the main floor, the divided and nerved vaults, reminiscent of the those in the crypt of the Colonia Güell, and the columns, topped by successive corbels, complement the windows with mitred arches, either single or composite with one, two or three dividers, much more slender than the largest ones seen in Gothic architecture.

Since the panoramic views were one of the principal attractions of the site, the main floor is situated on the first storey rather on the ground floor, and the bedrooms, informal sitting rooms and the attached services are supplemented by those in the half-basement.

Gaudí obtained a striking polychrome effect by taking advantage of the humble slate found on the site, giving four tones: dark grey, green, brown and light yellow, and he used them to face the brick walls and roofs. The qualities of this stone contrast with the jambs, partitions and arches of the large windows, where artificial granite and ceramics take on, by contrast, the quality of ivory.

The wrought iron gate at the main entrance, the uprights capped by lanceolate forms and the tympanum of the main door with the traditional salutation offered to visitors, are magnificent. Not so the door itself and handrails of the main stairway and terrace, which are not Gaudí's work.

Expressionist Naturalism

This period is characterised by a vitalist modernism born from the baroque spirit. Gaudí, however, was not content with the superficial character endowed by an external whirlwind, but instead imbues it with the vibration of a living being that, beginning with the structure and finishing with the plasticity, takes on a cosmic sense, even in the smallest details. It began with the decoration and ornamentation of the façade of the Sagrada Familia and in the Casa Calvet. In the upper church at the Colonia Güell he had used a geological naturalism also seen in the viaducts at Güell Park, which reached its peak in the Casa Batlló and the Casa Milà. The Bellesguard mansion, described above, and the completely new elements used in the restoration of Palma de Mallorca's Cathedral, represent a fusion of this style with the preceding style, moved by Gothic's heavy hand.

We have already seen that Gaudí seldom used sculpture in his secular projects. He also reduced it to a minimum in the apse of the Sagrada Familia. But when he needed to present and set the story of the Gospels – as in the Façade of the Nativity – he enthusiastically took up the task of creating a complex iconographic composition, set against an exuberant background of flora and fauna that, with a fundamentally baroque approach – overflows the territory of decoration and insinuates itself into the architecture. The fact is that Gaudí, although he had never had the opportunity to work in a Baroque style, had a definite preference for it. He heaped praise on the Bonifás sculptures in the sanctuary of Our Lady of Mercy in Reus. "I don't think that you could find more graceful statues anywhere in the world." When he went to the cathedral of Manresa to give advice on its restoration, he walked right by a magnificent 14th century retable to stop contentedly before a Baroque altar to Our Lady of the Rosary. He was familiar with the passionate *Transparente* in Toledo's Cathedral and loved to recount the skilful daring of Narciso Tomé. On one occasion he said to me: "I would have liked to receive a commission to build in Madrid, to create something to accompany the beautiful obelisks of the Toledo Bridge." He also admired the baroque window screens of the Belén church in Barcelona, since destroyed, and the filigree choir lectern in the church at San Juan de las Abadesas.

It should not surprise us, then, that he reached artistic maturity with the façade of the Sagrada Familia that he completed and with the Casa Calvet on Calle Caspe. But, as we have already mentioned, he was not content with the external dynamics of traditional Baroque, but instead multiplied its possibilities and looked nature full in the face, having exaggeration, allied to nerve, give forms a life that radiates outwards from the inside. He found in nature all of the basic rules for architectural elements: "Columns are tree trunks, roofs are mountains with their slopes and peaks, vaults are caves with their parabolic section. Harder layers of rock form lintels and corbels when the softer layers underneath are eroded." He observed the profusion of curved wrappings and gradual transitions between natural elements, indicating the point

Wrought-iron guard from the Façade of the Nativity (Sagrada Familia). The crib is held up by a palm-tree referring to the tree of Jesse, with the fronds gathered together by a banner engraved with names from Jesus' genealogy. To protect this delicate sculpture, the architect made this railing from continuous iron that winds in and around itself.

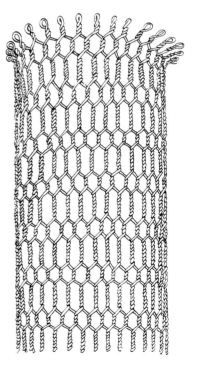

where fingers join as an example, saying, "Look, they are paraboloids," and "When you twist your forearm or your torso, you form helicoids." Thus, without descending into a puerile imitation totally at odds with architecture and owing to their evocative strength, everyone sees in the works belonging to this group living, natural forms: columns like elephants' feet, openings that look like lips, waves, rocky cliffs and the colours of the landscape.

It is interesting to note that this enthusiasm for naturalism coincided with his regret at having to give up his vacations on the family farm at Riudoms, with his hikes on Mallorca and his visits to that island's caves and with the publication in Spain of Ruskin's works, where we find concepts similar to those seen in Gaudí's works of the time. The last works included in this group have marked geological character, leading into his final period, where his architecture took on a living organic sense.

Casa Calvet (1898-1904). This elegant Baroque building, awarded the Barcelona City Council architecture prize, stands in Calle Caspe at number 48. It is a block of apartments, where the owner reserved for his own use an office and warehouses on the ground floor and the main floor with its gallery.

The façade is rusticated stone. On the lower level, the composition is centred on the gallery and higher it is articulated along two axes marked by trefoil balconies on corbels extending from the lintels below. These two axes are finally emphasised by the crowning gable ends that are gracefully pierced giving on to small and curiously formed cast iron balconies whose parapets and platforms are a single piece. Below the mouldings are seen the busts of the patron saints of the owner and of his home town and on the railings above, the martyrs' emblems. Above them all, balustraded feet support a metal cross. When the bases were being built, the Condesa Güell, who happened to be watching, asked Gaudí "What is that tangle?" he replied "Madam, it the Cross, which is a tangle and a nuisance for so many!"

The gallery is a marvel of decorative sculpture, particularly the corbel supporting it and its unique cupola. Here and in the wrought iron joints of the rails are to be found elements taken from the structure of mushrooms known as *múrgulas* or "devil's eggs". But the masterpiece of ironwork is to be found in the "bedbug" doorknobs, notable for the difficulty of their execution and their curious and symbolic decorative elements: a bedbug perched on a background of four grooves, which, when the doorknob is turned, is crushed by the Cross.

The stairway is especially noteworthy, with arches supported on fluted columns made of reinforced artificial granite, leading to courts through triple openings, also arched. The benches, set in spaces let into the walls to avoid narrowing the landings, the barrier enclosing the lift shaft and the banister, polychromed and gilded, the reinforced wood handrails and the grilles of the doors to the flats are all extremely original. Gaudí designed these grilles, which had remained unfinished, in a curiously expeditious manner. He took a handful of clay and placed it where a grille was to go. He modelled a convex surface and then pierced the mass by pushing the fingers of his right hand into it repeatedly, with a certain rhythm, until it was sufficiently open.

In the interiors, the decoration, based on woodwork, is supremely important. "When the plasterers were about to begin work on the ceilings, which were going to be heavily ornamented, they went on strike. In order to avoid the work being held up and in order to teach them a lesson, I decided to replace the planned ceilings with simple and shallow coffered ceilings." This obliged him to pay careful attention to the details on doors, with fine grooves, and to provide the frames with decorations that would make them seem larger, echoing the moulding of the doors themselves. He covered this magnificent woodwork with thousands of delicately painted flowers.

The woodwork furnishings in the owner's office and warehouse are a marvel of construction and good taste. The forms and shapes of the desk, bookcase and directors' chairs condense all of the delicacy of French Baroque, without succumbing to its arbitrariness. The desk, armchairs and seats are true museum pieces and their design follows a totally naturalistic concept, with seats and backs resembling pieces of shell and the joints between feet and uprights resembling living articulations. Their construction and assembly are masterful; a person sitting in them feels comfortably accommodated, with the just the right support for their lower back.

Upholstered furniture (Casa Calvet, Barcelona). From the parlour on the first floor of the house. They are covered in green silken velvet; their helicoidal gilt wooden legs are reinforced in flowered iron, also gilt, continuing and linking together to reinforce the chair-back.

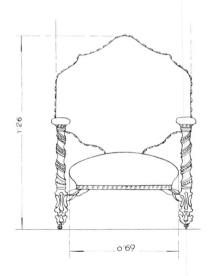

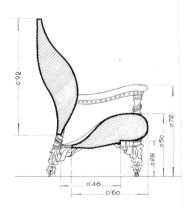

Crypt of the church at the Colonia Güell (1898-1914). As the crowning touch to his model development, the Colonia Güell, in Santa Coloma de Cervelló, its founder commissioned Gaudí to build a church. Unfortunately, only the crypt and the portico were built.

Chair and bench
(Casa Calvet, Barcelona).

Once the site, on a rise surrounded by pine groves, had been chosen and the measurements decided, Gaudí built a model, in the form of a mechanical skeleton. It was a polyfunicular interpretation of the building, made from cords with weights attached in proportion to the length of the cords and the load to be carried. He thus created an authentic organism, where the placement and axial form of each element was linked to and depended on every other element. In order to cover this skeleton, the usual geometric forms would have proved insufficient, even if they were handled with the his self-assured Baroque approach. He therefore decided to use curves, which offer flexibility of placement of the main elements. "When masons build a wall, they place two plumb uprights and string a line between them horizontally. If one of the uprights goes out of plumb, which happens much more often than you may think, the masons, believing that they are building a flat wall, are in fact making a paraboloid. We have gone directly and deliberately to this form and, seeing its beauty and the possibilities that it offers, we have also used it for the walls and vaults."

For the columns – all of them now decidedly inclined – he experimented with paraboloid shapes, which led him gradually towards helicoidal forms.

For the plasticity of the church's exterior, Gaudí, for the first time, took a naturalistic approach along tectonic orographic lines that, in this case, would have been evocative of Montserrat. He seems to have taken up Ruskin's enthusiasm: *To satisfy the human heart's thirst for the beauty of God's works is the highest purpose of the mountains*. The photographs of the model, given corporeal form by gluing strips of tissue paper to the cords, provide us with an idea of that plasticity. Colouring would also have been taken from the landscape: "A combination of burnt brick and concrete made with clinker and pyrites gives the lower walls the exact colour of the sandstone of the site. Higher up, the grey becomes more silvery, and closer to the colour of the trunks of the pine trees surrounding the building. Higher still, there would have been greens, purples and blues, done in glazed materials, matching the treetops, the mountaintops on the horizon and the sky itself."

The church has a ovoid plan and is divided into two parts: a crypt with a portico, taking advantage of the slope, and an upper chapel, approached by means of a stairway placed above the portico, as mentioned earlier. The interior of the crypt is divided into five naves: a central nave presided by the apse and the apsidal choir, and two on each side that join to become one at the door. To the left is the bell tower and to the right, the Christ Chapel. The columns are not aligned transversally, but instead, the ones dividing the side naves are displaced to allow better visibility of the altar from everywhere in the church.

Both in the portico and in the crypt, we find the first Gaudinian pillars, their tops taking the form of branching columns. The multitude of brick nerves converging on some of these pillars also gives them a palm-like appearance. The material depends on the load; the four supporting the central dome are basalt from Castellfollit de la Roca, with lead instead of mortar joints, to keep their section from being excessive, while the others are Garraf stone or worked bricks, in the case of those bearing the lightest loads. Work was carried out to specifications calculated from direct measurement of the cord model.

The windows, projecting from the inclined walls, are in the form of pointed louvers with parabolic hood moulds. Their glazing is protected by very fine grilles that are almost invisible, made from long, thin needles used in the textile industry at the Colonia. Over the lintel of the doorway is a ceramic composition comprising symbols of the four cardinal virtues: prudence is represented by a moneybox with a snake, justice by a balance and sword, fortitude by the warrior's helmet and breastplate and temperance by a knife cutting a loaf of bread and a *porrón* (a wine bottle with a conical drinking spout), since, as Gaudí said, "thanks to the *porrón*, our country is where you will find the fewest drunkards". The design of the double pews is striking, with their arched shape obliging the people sitting in them face away from each other, making eye contact or conversation difficult.

"If I had not been able to test the large-scale use of curved forms in the Colonia Güell, with helicoidal shapes in the columns and paraboloids in the walls and vaults, I would not

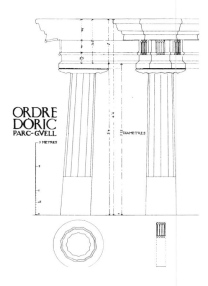

ORDRE
DORIC
PARC-GVELL

Doric columns (Güell Park, Barcelona). The park is laid out around a conical central valley, closed at the bottom by a semi-circular esplanade. The whole forms a Greek theatre with the city, the sea and the sky as backdrop. Gaudí chose an old-fashioned Doric hall of columns to hold up the esplanade. The silhouette of the entablature around the exterior columns gives way to the ceramic scallops of the bench-balustrade above the hall of columns, giving it a happy, folksy touch. The columns are 3.4 times the entablature, the latter being divided into 10.5 equal parts, of which five correspond to the cornice, three to the frieze and two-and-a-half to the architrave.

have dared to use them for the Sagrada Familia." This work, then, was the initial experiment for the architecture that Gaudí was to incorporate into the final phase of his masterpiece. The upper chapel would have been a monumental model of the naves and dome of the Sagrada Familia, and he was bitterly disappointed that they had not let him finish it.

This was undoubtedly the source of his basic ideas for the Casa Milà, which, aside from its outpouring of geological naturalism, was meant as a truly Marian monument.

Güell Park (1900-1914). This housing development project for the southern slope of the Montaña Pelada was commissioned by Conde Güell and later converted into a city park, connected to the Vallcarca park on the opposite side of the hill. The composition of this aristocratic garden city is centred on the conoid form of half of the slope, where Gaudí built a spacious plaza for entertainments, reminiscent of the stage of a Greek theatre, formed in part by levelling, with the rest supported by a handsome Doric colonnade, reached by a highly original staircase beginning just inside the main entry. A network formed by the broad central boulevard and the roadways for vehicles, with shortcuts in the form of footpaths, makes all of the areas of the sloping property easily accessible.

Radial terraces allow people to scatter all around the hillside surrounding the semi-circular plaza, as they would have done in an ancient amphitheatre. At the highest point of the property, a dry-stone plinth supporting the three Calvary crosses crowns the composition and at the same time serves as a viewpoint.

"When Doctor Torras i Bages went to visit the work being done at Güell Park, after strolling about for a while, with his head bent slightly forward, as he was short-sighted, he commented: "I can see that you have used the topography to attain the greatest possible convenience." Like all of the Bishop's comments, it was most appropriate; although he was physically short-sighted, his inner vision was crystal clear.

The ground here is rocky and therefore not suitable for trees. There was a shortage of materials for terracing and levelling was also difficult. Gaudí found the best and most elegant solution: the portico-viaduct, offering a sheltered walk in bad weather and cool shade in the summer. He built it using a minimum of materials and a maximum variety. It seems to have been born effortlessly from the earth. Gaudí put to use here what he had learned from the noteworthy dry-stone structures in his native Tarragona, expanding on techniques that are doubtless of prehistoric origin and turning them into architecture. "An ancient proverb says: 'Divide and rule' or, 'Divide and conquer'. We had to divide the prism of the ground to reduce the load, permitting retaining walls and porticoes at the lowest cost. So there are walls that are internally stepped, so that the load of ground on the steps confers greater stability. Other walls are isolated, surrounding volumes of ground in such a way that not only do they not transmit any thrust but the vertical load also reduces the projection of the buttresses to a minimum. In others, the placement of drains and sewers hollows out the prism and instead of having to support a terrace, they only support 'hollow' ground, etc. We followed the same approach in covering the porticoes. Rather than few supports and large vaults, many supports that divided the vaults up into small sections, eliminating the need for expensive domes and making construction easier."

The adoption of balanced forms, with the accompanying inclined pillars, allows bearing sections to be reduced to a minimum, helped at times by the weight of strategically placed balconies and plant pots. In the porticoes with three rows of columns, those of the middle row are, logically, vertical, as are all of the inner columns of the platform of the central plaza, while the outer ones, which support the pediment moulded in a Baroque manner, are inclined. This gives them an undulating outline, crowned by a serpentine bench finished in ceramics. The lions' heads, with the open mouths serving as drains and the mutules and triglyphs of the pediment are radically naturalist, in realistic forms totally devoid of geometry. With the use of modified echinus mouldings in the necking and small curved beams following equal resistance curves between the columns this grand colonnade creates a singular effect, where the capitals seem raised into the roof and shafts of the columns seem to penetrate into the capitals.

In the entrance pavilions and the surrounding walls, the gleaming ceramic facing of the roofs and terraces contrasts with rugged severity of the masonry, which is accentuated by the use of protruding stones.

The housing development was unsuccessful and only a few plots were sold and built up. The chapel that Gaudí wanted to built for the residents would have been redundant and it is therefore not so regrettable that it was substituted by the simple Calvary mount mentioned above. Likewise, the large cistern to provide water for cleaning purposes and for watering the residents' private gardens, and the area meant to house the market, located under the platform of the amphitheatre, were never necessary.

Leaving aside the decoration of the Marqués de Castelldosrius' house, on Calle Mendizábal number 19 (now Calle Nueva Junta de Comercio), on the occasion of the wedding Conde Güell's oldest daughter, the railings of the Miralles house, a project that was not at all well carried out, since Gaudí left it in the hands of one of his assistants, the renovation of the main floor of the building at Calle Puertaferrisa number 3 when the Marqués de Castelldosrius and his family moved there, and the picturesque attractions done for the Sala Mercè, in which Gaudí created the most fantastic settings, and also leaving aside various non-architectural works, we must mention, as one of his minor works during this period, the monumental First Glorious Mystery of the rosary, at Montserrat (1904).

Gaudí placed it on a bend in the trail and excavated the funerary cave and the empty sepulchre realistically in the rock face; to the left of the Sepulchre are the Holy Women being told by the angel of Christ's resurrection. When the spectator turns, they receive the moving vision of the resplendent Christ that seems to rise up from the middle of the high crag on that side. The sculptures inside the cave are stone figures by Renart and the figure of Christ, in gilt bronze, is by Llimona.

In order to provide better vision of the grouping and to allow greater numbers of people to gather, the trail was widened and fenced with a bench and railing. "Now all that remains is to plant small trees and humble vegetables, to evoke the orchard of the Good Gardener spoken of in the scriptures, and so that birdsong will accompany the Easter Dawn Mass." A beautiful wrought iron gate guards the entrance to the cave.

The Mystery was dedicated with Maragall's exquisite words, reproduced on a bronze plaque: "The spiritual league of Our Lady of Montserrat, in the name of the piety of Catalonia, offers up this mystery, the sign of all resurrection." It was the last mystery to be built and the most expensive, but also the most interesting.

Restoration of Palma de Mallorca's Cathedral (1900-1914). It was not a renovation, but a restoration, and not in the strict sense of recreating elements from a specific style or era and sacrificing those of other eras, but of putting things back in their place and recovering their true function. It was therefore an architectural and liturgical restoration, a Herculean work within King Jaime's Cathedral, one that inevitably exasperated minor archaeologists with no artistic sense who favour the mummification of works of art. "The co-existence of different styles is fitting for the Church, since it shows the homage of the spirit down the ages." In this way, he made use of Plateresque and Baroque elements, freely adapting them to the construction of pews and cantor's seats and did not hesitate to imbue the Cathedral's Gothic atmosphere with the spirit of modernity. "We should practise architecture without archaeology. What is important above all is the relationship between things, their arrangement. So, we should not copy forms, because forms of a specific character may be made by possessing their spirit." We see him achieve the essentially Gothic four-lobed shapes simple by twisting a handrail, produce plinths and canopies in the same style but with a total freedom of moulding, and unite Plateresque and Baroque with new elements in complete harmony.

This sweeping rearrangement of valuable works of art in order to put things in their proper place and order them strictly according to their liturgical function could only have been undertaken by a bishop of Don Campins' standing, and his own talent led him to choose the man with the extraordinary ability to carry out that undertaking even more effectively than he had imagined.

The Gothic choir, with its Plateresque *iube*, was removed from the centre of the nave, thus restoring its overall unity. The handsome Gothic retable behind the high altar, which blocked the view and the use of the Bishop's throne, was moved. The Mudejar gallery, called the gallery of the candles, which broke the vertical lines of the presbytery walls, was eliminat-

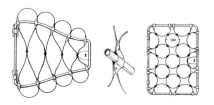

Railings (Palma de Mallorca cathedral). They flank the side entries to the presbytery. Their decoration is unusual, using flat iron circumferences linked by tubes.

Chandelier (Palma de Mallorca cathedral). Wrought flat bars of iron. Simple twists produce the four lobes so typical of the Gothic, without the intricacies of the genuine medieval articles.

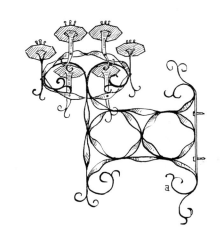

Stool (Casa Batlló, Barcelona). An unusual piece of furniture from a dressing room. The legs rest on the ground directly below the angles of the seat, providing it with perfect stability.

Chair (Casa Batlló, Barcelona). The chair's shape reminds one of a mollusc's valves; it is comfortable to sit in.

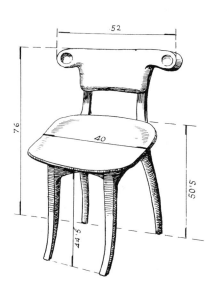

ed. The blocked windows piercing these walls were opened once again to the light and two of them were provided with glazing – one dedicated to the confessors and one to the virgins – done using the advanced techniques described above. The apse was restored, with the Bishop's throne and the high chapel, called the Trinity Chapel, and the royal sarcophagi were once again visible. Also, taking into account the length of the choir stalls, the special dispensation for co-celebrant priests to use them during pontifical masses, and the need to have the cantor's seats near the altar, Gaudí extended the new presbytery, bringing it as far as the first row of columns of the nave.

However, the valuable elements that had been removed were not relegated to a place among a distracting array of museum pieces. Instead, they were respectfully used in the Cathedral itself. The Plateresque door from the back of the choir was placed as an elegant triumphal arch at the entry to the All Saints Chapel; the Gothic retable, divided to form a two-storey gallery and supported on large stone corbels, adorns the extensive wall above the Mirador Portal; its central image, of the Virgin and Child, occupies the place of honour in the Trinity Chapel; the splendid figures of the saints, under slender canopies, were aptly placed above the doors leading from the presbytery to the adjoining rooms, and the Plateresque finial elements from the choir were used in the supports of the new cantor's seats. The interesting pulpits, also Plateresque, were also re-used, but situated differently so that the larger one is used for reading the Gospel and the smaller one for reading from the Epistles.

The Gothic Bishop's throne was restored to magnificent surroundings, with a pictorial ceramic backdrop showing the Bishop's coats of arms. On both sides are the two rows of choir stalls, since "when the Chapters act without the Bishop, they are as if headless, and can do nothing worthy". Alone in the centre is the high altar, unadorned, with no predella, accompanied only by the four curtain columns. It is covered by an ample antique brocade tapestry baldachin, below which hangs the most audacious candelabrum imaginable, both of them suspended from the high vault.

This solemn grouping is flanked by the seats for the numerous celebrants, the porticoes and galleries for the cantors, and the Plateresque pulpits, vigorously topped by sounding boards and spires bearing symbols alluding to the readings given from them. The culminating point of the presbytery is a magnificent iron rastrellum, with a sliding inner door. In the middle of the nave, as a trophy from the no longer extant synagogue, hangs the menorah, with hundreds of tiny light bulbs. At the back of the apse, in the peak of the arch leading to the high altar, Gaudí deliberately placed an answering figure, in the forma of a tiara with a triple crown of gilt iron with tiny light bulbs the colour of topaz.

The project that Gaudí left for the royal tombs in the high chapel, in the form of a model as original as it is excessively theatrical, was never begun. He also left studies for figures of the Holy Trinity and the Assumption, to adorn the high chapel. The lamp was never finished in its definitive form and materials, with these only present on one side; worth noting is the totally naturalistic treatment of its gilt spikes.

The colouring of the high backs of the choir stalls was also left barely begun. They had become very dark with age and did not harmonise with the marvellous ceramic decoration of the wall that was their backdrop, consisting of a rain of drops of blood, sprinkled with sparkling pieces, and with an inscription of a fragment from the Gospels: "His blood upon us". The canons had objected to the choice of text, which they thought might provoke ironic commentaries, and they wanted to have the full text used. Gaudí defended his choice, saying: "Monumental texts and inscriptions must always be fragmentary, because they only serve as a reminder for the erudite," and finished defending his position: "The sacraments are the food of life, the texts are medicine, and we could say that the Gospels are a dispensary. You are like someone who goes to a pharmacy and asks for a prescription for food." Shortly afterwards, a relative of Doctor Campins was responsible for the reading and he chose a text from St. John Chrysostom where the Holy Scriptures are referred to as medicine for the soul.

Gaudí took advantage of the work in the Cathedral to study, along with Rubió, the stability of the building and to remedy the distortion of the daring columns, correcting their disquieting optical slenderness with lighting rings. These, along with the candleholders of the curtain columns, are beautiful examples of ironwork.

Casa Batlló (1904-1906). The manufacturer Batlló commissioned Gaudí to renovate the building on Paseo de Gracia at number 43. The entry vestibule is to one side of the façade, leading to the door and stairway to the main floor, reserved for the owner, and along the side is the stairway leading to the upper floors, each one divided into two apartments.

The private stairway leading to the main floor leads to a reception room, containing a dignified fireplace. This gives access to the row of rooms across the façade, with the sitting room in the middle, presided by the oratory. This salon was connected to the side rooms by means of doorways furnished with folding wooden doors. These doors could be folded away to create one magnificent salon running the length of the façade and lit by one continuous gallery. In the row of rooms across the back of the building were the kitchen, in the middle, and bedrooms on either side. In between the front and back areas, lit from the interior courts and the stair well, were the remaining bedrooms and the service and bath rooms. The dining room gave onto an ample terrace, set with plant pots and a large parabolic sun shade. The arches of the attic are also parabolic, as are the frames of the skylights and the openings of the galleries on the façade, which have been said to resemble mouths that cannot close because of the toothpick that they have between their lips.

The rental apartments were not renovated to such a great extent and they have a normal layout.

On the façade, the continuous gallery of the main floor and two side galleries of the first floor are made from worked stone, in forms that take the Baroque of the Casa Calvet a step further. Both the architectural elements – jambs, arches and dividers – and the decorative elements are immensely naturalistic. Those with geological forms appear sculpted by water, as Ruskin would have said, and the organic ones look as if they had been conceived or taken root and grown there on the others. A sort of germination seems to burst forth in leaves, flowers, fruit, winged shapes, muscle– and bone-like volumes, furrows and festoons that call to mind moss and rivulets.

The stone foundation initiates the serpentine, undulating form that echoes the composition of the Casa Milà, which we will discuss below. The pale grey stone contrasts with the bright polychrome of the rest of the façade, which terminates in a gable end broken by a change of plane giving rise to a small tower of homage to the Holy Family and the Cross. Behind this gable end, a baroque and picturesque hummock, sheathed in ceramic scales, forms the roof of the building's attics. The outline of the gable end and ridge takes on the appearance of a backbone and the raised body of the hummock evokes a crustacean's shell, bringing to memory the parallel between the mountains and living creatures observed by the disciple of naturalism.

The mensular stones of the balconies and their rail of curved cast iron plaques, adorned with shells carrying wrought iron overlays, complete the work's rhythmically undulating volumes.

The glass and ceramic polychromy of the façade is like a synthesis of the most beautiful bucolic visions, with the purples and siennas of the mountain hovering over all the shades of fields and dew, in the morning light. It gives an impression of life that brings to mind Ruskin's connection between the brightness of colour and the vigour of life, which, as we have already seen, was seconded by Gaudí, and it reveals such a sensation of ingenuous optimism that it caused one English architect to exclaim: "It looks like the house in Hansel and Gretel!", a comment that greatly pleased Gaudí.

The ingenious method that Gaudí applied to control the colours used on the façade is of great technical interest. It was based on ceramic discs in three different sizes with the basic colours that had been chosen painted around their edges, which Gaudí placed himself. Following this guiding sketch, the workmen placed pieces of glass with the same colour, growing progressively less intense until they were diluted by the pale greys of the background.

In the woodwork of the balconies, glazing, main stairway and oratory, he obtained the "play of light" using curved walls, reducing moulding, which was unnecessary, to nothingness. The forms here are more precise and less virtuoso than in the Casa Calvet, taking on the shapes of valves and petals.

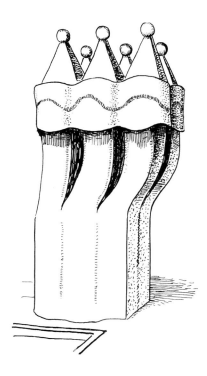

Chimneys (Casa Batlló, Barcelona). Strange constructions of long, curved, thin bricks covered in ceramic and glass. The helical twist is the same as that found in flames and whirlwinds.

Ventilation shaft (Casa Milà, Barcelona).
The wavy surfaces and openings in the
centre of each facet, give the impression
of an eye without a pupil.

Group of chimneys
(Casa Milà, Barcelona).
The helical arrangement
of the chimneys and the
combination of the twists
with the cowls topping
them off produce warriors
helmets with eye openings.

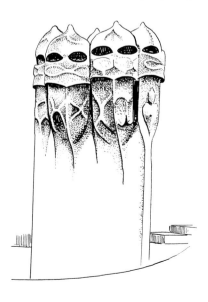

The candlesticks, twisted like roots, and the crucifix in the oratory were outstanding, particularly the crucifix, made by the sculptor Mani following Gaudí's instructions. In this piece, he reiterated in real terms the torture of the crucifixion, in contrast to the "dancing" Christs traditionally depicted by painters and sculptures. The arms are almost vertical, holding up the victim, who, supported by the foot block, has his knees pointing outwards and his legs painfully bent. The architect had these works reproduced for the high altar of the crypt of the Sagrada Familia.

The house commissioned to Gaudí by the painter Graner and which did not get past the preliminary stages, was conceived in the same plastic and polychrome style as the Casa Batlló.

Casa Milà (1906-1910). Located at Paseo de Gracia number 92, it forms a huge mass that covers the whole of the chamfered corner and a sizeable stretch of the block on Calle Provenza and is in fact two buildings. It was commissioned by Rosario Segimón de Milà.

The artist, thoroughly caught up in architectural elaboration and moved by his Marian devotion, conceived the work as a monument to the Our Lady of the Rosary, since "Barcelona does not have enough monuments". And foreseeing the tremendous cost of such an ambitious project, he decided to make savings on the construction itself: "The Casa Milà is constructed with great economy, taking the best advantage of the materials used, to give it strength." Thus in the structure of pillars and main beams – since there are no bearing walls – he took great care with the connection of these elements, in order to reduce their sections. The beams supporting the row of rooms along the façade were also lightened and project on the outside; the rooftop attic and its access structures are built of thin stepped platforms and double partition arches. Even the façade, which gives the impression of being an indestructible pile of stone blocks, to the extent of originating its nickname, La Pedrera, is mostly thin sheets of Vilafranca limestone, an easily workable material, and the minimal amount of iron used would frighten many technicians.

The façade's undulations create apertures with diverse orientations whose large size considerably reduces the weight of the walls. The numerous windows inside and out and the internal structure using only pillars allowed the apartments to be laid out according to their residents' requirements and, if necessary, to change the function of the whole building. Gaudí said to us: "I wouldn't be surprised if this building were converted sometime in the future into a grand hotel, considering how easy it is to alter layouts and the large number of bathrooms."

The many projecting beams gave rise to the undulations of the façade's parapets that serve at the same time as shades for the openings below. These undulations are made with parabolic arches that, in joining the lines of the parapets and lintels by straight lines and curves, give varying parabolic surfaces. The variations in width of the attic give rise to differing heights for the parabolic arches sustaining it, producing a final double undulation. The continuity and relief of the parapets give the façade's plasticity a sense of stratification.

Gaudí created an architectural transcription of the Fran Guerau gorge, which he had admired on his hikes. It gives the impression that an irresistible geological force carved this enormous block, leaving it with a reminder of movement; the bond with forms of nature is complete. The ensemble constitutes a monumental plinth that was meant to support a magnificent sculpted grouping, in stone, gilt metal and glass, representing the Virgin and two angels advancing over Barcelona. This explains the inclusion in each of the façade's upper crests of one word of the Salve Regina.

Polychromy on the façade is limited to the contrast between the yellowish stone and the white marble facing of the attic and the marble and ceramic mosaic, also white, of the structures giving access to the rooftop, which provide a gleaming backdrop, half snow, half cloud, for the sculpture that was never made. Gaudí looked to nature to complete the shading. "The patina of the stone, enriched by the flowers and climbing plants on the balconies, will give the building a constantly changing array of colours." Indeed, he had planned for places to plant them and a system for watering them. The rails of balconies and verandas were originally painted the colours of roots, leaves and flowers, providing an attractive complement. Here too, the architect seems to echo Ruskin's thoughts: *Vegetation is the way that the earth makes herself into man's companion, his friend and his teacher*.

In contrast to the façade, in the interior Gaudí evoked mostly marine impressions and themes. For the floors, he made beautiful, light green hexagonal tiles, with lightly engraved winkles, and on the ceilings he drew octupi and marine plants, with the surface of the water rippled by the wind, the spirals traced in whirlpools and garlands of sea froth on the beach. There is no lack of other Marian references, which he wanted to permeate the entire work, in emotive inscriptions on the Virgin's ages and the events of her life. Unfortunately, many of these have been removed and of the others, only a few words remain. But there is one very beautiful entire sentence, referring to the Virgin's childhood. Around one rosette, adorned with tiny flowers and stars, read the words: "Oh Mary, do not be troubled that you are small, for the flowers and stars are also small."

It is a shame that this work should have gone unfinished, not only because of the absence of the sculptures that would have justified it, but also because most of the finishing touches - door frames, many rails and some fireplaces and ceilings – were abandoned by Gaudí. Many fireplaces were left without their broken ceramic finish, as were the entrance vestibules and courts, which were succinctly painted with frescoes by Ivo Pascual, who had worked with Gaudí in Mallorca.

Although he went beyond the bounds of architecture, by moving it into an imitative area, signalling the end of his period of expressionist naturalism, this building, particularly its attic and the upper volumes embellishing it, marks the beginning of his development of a new and entirely organic concept of architectural creation. This is why we have included it here, as a transitional work in Gaudí's final phase.

The Casa Milà has always been Gaudí's most controversial work. There is nevertheless one fact on which all will agree, indicating its worth: it reduces the surrounding works to insignificance; the spectator is spellbound by the intense contrast of the light as it pours down its magical walls.

Organic Synthesis

We have come to the final period, a progression past the preceding one, where function, both utilitarian and spiritual, structural frame and expressive plasticity are all totally and mutually interdependent, as in nature, where function creates the organ.

In artistic terms, it represents the architectural integration of the structural plasticity of natural entities, the substitution of the column as a tree trunk by the column as a tree. Ruskin's observation that we cannot help but notice the coincidences between beautiful architecture and the structure of trees, became a guiding principle for Gaudí, who, when an artist asked him where he had learned this new architecture, pointed to tree near his workshop, saying: "There is my teacher."

In his prime, and rich in accumulated experience, Gaudí once again encountered the pureness of imagery of the child enthralled by nature, and turned it to the service of religious art, embroidered on a complex mechanical and geometrical fabric. Upon entering this period of Gaudinian genius, we should recall the words that Plato had inscribed in stone over the entrance to the Akademos: Let no one enter here who does not know geometry.

Sagrada Familia schools (1909). Located on the grounds of the Sagrada Familia, where the main façade of the church was to be built, Gaudí built them with the simplest materials.

They follow the wholly organic concept of the attic of the Casa Milà, but, where the latter's structure consists of stepped platforms on diaphragm arches with a perimeter of sheathed double partition walls, in this case the roof platforms are continuous and rest on wooden beams of varying inclination supported by the longitudinal main beam. The roof has a single slope and drains towards both of the main façades. The façades are built as double diaphragms with the brick exposed. Rigidity is obtained by means of undulations that counteract the thrust from the movement of the beams.

It is unfortunate that the curved surfaces of the roof and the bascule beams are hidden by the ceilings, and without the proper ventilation, they will not last as long as they should. It is also unfortunate that the perimeter walls are hidden behind vertical partitions that, besides being unsightly, reduce the size of the classrooms.

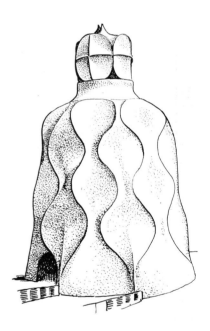

Stair entrances (Casa Milà, Barcelona). The stairways leading from the attics to the roof are covered with a variety of daring, domed shapes made of brick covered with marble chips.
These booths or monumental markers, some topped by four-armed crosses, were to attend a statue of Our Lady accompanied by two angels that Gaudí planned for the top of the façade.

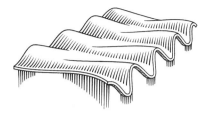

Wavy roof of flat thin brick
(Temporary schools of
the Sagrada Familia, Barcelona).

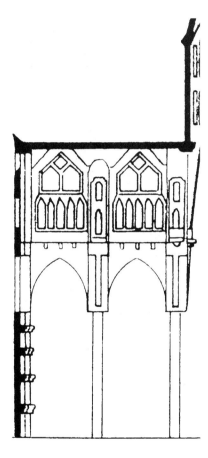

Section in Gothic style
(Sagrada Familia, Barcelona).
The first plan for the aisles involved
pointed arches; the architect's ideas
relating to construction already saw
them as being very slim – as in
the entrance hall of the Bishop's Palace
in Astorga – which would allow them
to be narrower and give less thrust.
In order to lighten them further,
he designed openings in the walls,
letting more light into the church.
The columns are cylindrical, without
the medieval accessories.

Gaudí emphasised the geometric treatment of plastic elements and began using heli-coidal surfaces, although they were still derived from parabolic curves.

With the suspension of funding, the final work on the Façade of the Nativity came almost to a complete standstill (1914). The architect sold property of his beloved family home to reduce the deficit. Disappointed at being unable to finish the Casa Milà and being informed of the decision of Conde Güell's heirs not to continue construction of the church at the Colonia, he decided not to accept any further commissions and to dedicate himself entirely to applying his new organic approach to the naves and façades planned for the Sagrada Familia, abandoning the dangerous direction of imitation and returning totally to the geometric sense of classical architecture.

After four years of constant, step by step pursuit of perfection in his design, he arrived at the final, arborescent form of the naves and the definitive resolution of the columns. During a pause in this avid search, he drew up the final design for the composition of the Façade of the Passion, the culmination and ultimate expression of the paraboloidism of the Colonia Güell. He then began on the model for the church's main façade, the Façade of Life, and the model for the sacristies. The model for the sacristies was completed and was a foretaste of his plans for the domes. The third model for the naves, based entirely on paraboloids, evolved gradually into the fourth model, showing that he was not afraid of breaking the plastic or static unity in abandoning the concept of a single mechanical force, with the incorporation of simple helicoids and hyperboloids.

In the nave columns, paraboloids are relegated to a secondary position, as transitional elements joining helicoids and hyperboloids. With a further six years of gruelling effort, he managed to resolve columns, vaults, lanterns, windows and roofs in an architectural accomplishment outstanding for its novelty, solidity and originality – all in keeping with pure Mediterranean classicism – and constituting unquestionably Gaudí's masterpiece.

He was right in claiming that "the history of architecture is the history of the temple," and we could add that the history of the column is the history of styles. The Gaudinian column is totally representative of the architect's true and definitive style, and has its precedents in all of the great classical styles. "It is tapered, pointed, inclined and grooved like the Doric column, and helicoidal, like some medieval and Baroque columns. As it rises, the grooves multiply and thin, reducing its section to a circle." This result is obtained, with extraordinary simplicity, by means of a star-shaped polygon with blunted points revolving in two opposite directions as it ascends. "The stars follow their orbit, which is their path of equilibrium; at the same time, they revolve, making their movement helicoidal. The columns of the Sagrada Familia follow an axis of force, the path of their stability, their equilibrium. It is generated on the basis of a star-shaped section revolving as it moves. Its movement is therefore also helicoidal, like the movement in tree trunks. The stars advance and retreat, since their orbits are closed circles. The column advances and retreats, because its movement is helicoidal and double, the revolutions are in two directions. All decoration of columns in all styles conforms, to a greater or lesser or degree, to the application of this principle."

He also resolved the most difficult of problems posed by architectural structure, the superposition of columns, complicated here by the insertion of small secondary columns near the main columns and where they join with the vaults, in the form of false *mushrooms*.

THE MASTERPIECE

In describing the architect's different works, we have made reference to elements of his crowning religious creation, which he was building at the same time, and to his application of all of his artistic achievements and techniques to the Sagrada Familia. We have also seen how, during his later periods, he resolutely undertook commissions in a spirit of experimentation.

Since this is Gaudí's most widely-known work, we will simply complete here our earlier references to the Sagrada Familia.

Significant Dates

On the last day of 1881, the Spiritual Association for Devotion to Saint Joseph, persuaded by their founder, José María Bocabella, purchased the property where the Sagrada Familia was to be built. It is bordered by Calles Mallorca, Marina, Provenza and Cerdeña, making it the largest block in the Barcelona's Ensanche. Gaudí, showing us a map of the city's current and future boundaries, with notes giving the distance between the farthest points, remarked: "Everything about the Sagrada Familia is providential. It is situated in the centre of the city and of the plain where Barcelona stands. It is the same distance from the church to sea as it is to hills, to Sants and to San Andrés, and to the Besós and Llobregat rivers."

On Saint Joseph's feast day in 1882, the first stone was laid of the church planned by the Diocese's architect, Francisco de P. del Villar. As a friend and former assistant of the architect, Gaudí attended the ceremony, little suspecting that not long afterwards, at the recommendation of Joan Martorell, a member of the Building Committee, he would be commissioned to build the church, of which only the crypt had been excavated and the supporting elements built up to half height.

Gaudí took charge of the project on November 3rd 1883 and, in order to take advantage of the work already done, he redrafted it following the long axis already laid out Villar, running parallel to Calle Marina. The new architect pointed out that he would have preferred to place the axis diagonally, giving the church a liturgically appropriate orientation, with the apse to the east and at the same time allowing it greater length. To gain the desired length, Gaudí placed the stairway leading up to the principal façade outside the site, on the other side of Calle Mallorca, covering a 65 metre stretch of the street.

The first chapel finished in the crypt was the central one in the apse, dedicated to Saint Joseph. Its altar is Romanesque and it was consecrated on the Saint's feast day in 1885. A provisional high altar was set up at the far end, for the cult of the Holy Family. The crypt was finished in 1891.

Following the usual progression in this type of construction, Gaudí continued building the walls and the spires of the apse, finished in 1893. Then he went on to build the north window of the transept, where the cloister begins, with the Door of the Rosary (1897) and the adjacent north-east façade, to which he dedicated himself intensely from 1891 until 1900.

In 1914, work came to a halt owing to lack of funds and Gaudí took up the revision of plans and models for the naves, continually reworking them. In 1917 he produced the final draft of the Façade of the Passion and began planning the model for the Façade of Life. He left off working on this to put the finishing touches to the plans for the naves and the models for the sacristies (1925). He was killed just when he had finished the initial plan for the Chapel of the Assumption, since lost.

Seven months prior to his death, he had seen one of the bell towers, the one dedicated to Saint Barnabas, completed.

Functional Aspects

Gaudí's plan was basilical, with five longitudinal naves and a transept with three naves, forming a short Latin cross, and a main dome covering the crossing of the two. Faithful to the local Gothic style, he made the side naves very high in proportion to the central nave.

The church, not counting the portico and vestibule, is the same length as the cathedral of Barcelona. The central nave is approximately as wide as that of the basilica of Santa María del Mar and the side naves are somewhat wider than that church's. The side naves are slightly lower than the Santa María del Mar's central nave, and the central nave is half again as high as the side naves. The outside naves, like the apse, have a gallery halfway up.

Next to the vestibule, the church is completed by two large chapels, one for baptisms and one for penitence. On either side of the apse are the sacristies and beneath it, the crypt. A peripheral cloister allows circumambulation of the church.

Gaudí's workshop
(Sagrada Familia).
The master's plain desk, the cupboards and upper shelves, the place he kept his plans and the worktops where Gaudí's assistants drew. The walls and ceiling are covered in models, plans and casts of a realism that impressed the visitor.

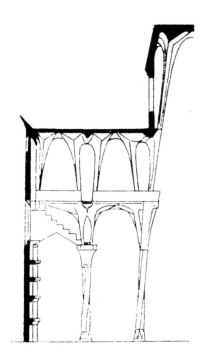

Parabolic section
(Sagrada Familia, Barcelona).
Parabolic arches have replaced the
lancet arches, the openings in the walls
have been unified and the arches are
beginning to turn into palm-leaves.
The columns are polygonal in cross-
section, with their faces all twisting
spirally in a single direction;
the window-openings and vaults
are also paraboloid, too.

The ample presbytery is circled behind by a lateral nave forming an ambulatory, and concentrically, seven subsidiary chapels and two stairways leading to the crypt and the triforia. "In the cathedral of Barcelona, the stairway down to the crypt is located in the central nave. This placement became fashionable and was used in other Gothic cathedrals. But it is a mistake and the proof is that, on the major feast days, they have to cover the stairway with a platform, so in the Sagrada Familia, instead of a central stairway, we made two lateral ones at the corners of the apse and the transept."

The main façade, spanning the five naves, and the two façades of the transept, have four bell towers each. The two tallest of the main façade are almost as tall as those of Cologne's Cathedral and the shorter ones are some twelve metres taller than the cupola of the Escorial, which was formerly the tallest monumental building in Spain. The central dome is twenty metres taller than the lantern on the cupola of St. Peter's in Rome, and the four towers flanking it are seven metres taller.

There is a half-basement, occupied by workshops, schools and facilities for charitable work, extending to the full surface area of the cloister, side naves, vestibule, chapels and sacristies.

The placement of all of these elements is strictly liturgical, in harmony with the performance of the rites of worship and with the basic tenets of Catholicism. The monumental vestibule of the main façade leads to the baptismal chapel, through which the neophytes pass into temple, and to the chapel of penitence, where sinners cleanse themselves before entering. There are another five doors into the church; situated near the two farthest doors are stairways to the galleries for female singers, as in the primitive basilicas. These lead to galleries in the vestibule, with room for five hundred singers, allowing them to take part in rites performed in the portico. The gallery over the ambulatory is for the boys' choir, with a capacity for seven hundred, whose voices will carry on a dialogue with the choir of priests. In lofts placed between the pillars supporting the main dome, there will be four organs and an area for the church's own musicians, who will complement the boys' and women's choirs and guide the faithful in the liturgy.

Between the singers' galleries and the longitudinal and transverse naves, there is room for fourteen hundred worshippers, with seats and kneelers.

Under the section equivalent to the triumphal arch, at the edge of the transept, is the altar, raised on a platform two metres above the floor of the church. The altar stands on a chamfered dais, reached by three steps. The presbytery is completed by the priests choir, situated behind the altar at a level halfway between the floor and the altar. This arrangement, besides emphasising the hierarchy of faithful and celebrants, allows a clear view of the altar. Above it are the candelabrum and baldachin, and a large Crucifix.

Didactic Aspects

One afternoon, I found Gaudí sitting at his desk with an open notebook, and he showed it to me, saying: "Do you see? Here on this page is the whole Christian doctrine." And it was true. It was a synoptic chart, covering not even half the page, giving all of the basic concepts related in an ingenious manner: the three Persons of the Trinity, corresponding to the three theological virtues and the first three Commandments, the seven sacraments, related to the seven entreaties of the Lord's Prayer, the seven days of Creation with the seven Commandments referring to our neighbour, the seven gifts of the Holy Spirit with the seven cardinal virtues and the seven opposing sins, the seven works of spiritual charity and the seven works of temporal charity, the Beatitudes corresponding to a rewording of the gifts of the Holy Spirit and the articles of the Creed, arranged synoptically. In a similar style, on other pages were notes on iconography and symbolism, correspondences between the Old and New Testaments and a sort of diagram of the various phases of the liturgical year, with a selection of their characteristic events and texts. All of them with accompanying notes as to their plastic representation.

This was the basis for what we could call the church's spiritual functionalism, the perfection of the ancient concept of decoration and adornment of the House of God as a didactic complex, the Bible of the people, as well as a worthy embellishment.

On the outside of the church, Gaudí unfolded a grand plastic representation of the Redemption of man by Jesus, and on the inside a vision the Church, Jesus' inseparable spouse, continuing the work of Redemption by means of its teachings and its sacramental blessings, all surrounding the re-enactment of the Sacrifice.

Domes, towers and bell towers. Above the crossing of the transept and nave is the central dome, dedicated to the Saviour. The Redeeming Victim is represented by the Lamb, placed in the centre of the crowning cross. The cross, brilliant with mosaics and glass shimmering in the sun, will project four beams into the night on solemn festivities, a guiding light, fulfilling Jesus' words, *I am the Light of the world*. This great dome is flanked by four towers, dedicated to the evangelists and topped by their winged symbols: man, lion, ox and eagle; two beams of light will shine from each, one towards the Lamb, who we know through the light of the Gospels, and one towards the ground, to show men the way.

Behind the main dome is a slightly smaller one, over the apsidal cupola, dedicated to the co-redemptrix, the Virgin Mary, and crowned with her symbol the morning star.

The twelve bell towers that call the faithful to the Church are dedicated to the apostles. Each one is topped with the bishops' symbols, the mitre with the cross and crosier, with a sculpture of the apostle on the front. From their peaks, two beams of light will shine, as from the evangelists' towers.

On the front of the apsidal spires and the windows of the naves, there will be statues of the workers in the vineyards of the Lord, the Saints who founded religious orders. The lanterns of the apsidal chapels will be carved with the seven messianic invocations sung at Christmas, set inside a large "o", since all of them begin thus: O Wisdom! (a lion's head and a lamb), O Lord! (crown and sceptre), O Stock of Joseph! (a spikenard), O Key of David! (a key with two teeth) O East! (the sun), O King of Nations! (cornerstone, with the initials of Christ crowned), and O Emmanuel (the tablets of the Law and a sword, before the royal mantle).

Inscriptions complete the meanings of the symbols. At the foot of the cross on the high dome are inscribed the words *Amen* and *Hallelujah;* at the top of the bell towers, *Hosanna in Excelsis*, halfway up, Sanctus, repeated three times, and nearer the base, *Sursum corda*. At the base, beside the statues of the apostles, are their names, from left to right, Barnabas, Simon, Judas Thaddeus and Matthew, on the Façade of the Nativity; James the Younger, Bartholomew, Thomas and Philip on the Façade of the Passion; Andrew, Peter, Paul and James the Elder on the Façade of Life. A little lower, at the corners of the bell towers are the names of Jesus, Mary and Joseph, against a background of palmettes. The clouds floating among the towers of the main façade will be carved with the words of the Creed.

Façades. Just as the higher parts of the church constitute a monument to the Redeemer and his helpers, the façades show the three great acts of the Redemption: Nativity, Ministry and Death, related to the three Persons of the Trinity and their attributes. The façade lit by the rising sun is dedicated to the Nativity and to the mystery of the Incarnation, a work of the Father's omnipotence. The main façade, illuminated by the midday sun, shows Jesus' Ministry, revealing the Son's wisdom. And on the façade facing the setting sun, are shown the Passion, Death and Resurrection of the Redeemer, revealing the Paraclete's infinite love.

The façades of the transept have three doorways, leading to the three naves. The scenes from the Gospels sculpted here are grouped according to the three theological virtues, Faith, Hope and Charity. As Charity is the most important, it is placed with the central door.

The Façade of the Nativity, also called the Joyous Façade, is a Christmas triptych framed in icicles. It shows the advent of Jesus, his birth and childhood and therefore includes all of the joyous mysteries of the Rosary, completed with the crowning of the Virgin Mary in glory.

The large central door, corresponding to the virtue of Charity, is composed around the manger, where the ox and the mule keep watch over the divine Child. It is supported by a column giving the Messiah's genealogy, dividing the doorway in half. Above, in the pierced tympanum is the bright star of the Magi; in the archivolts are the shepherds and the Magi adoring the Christ Child and higher up, angels playing musical instruments and others announcing the birth of Christ. Just above the star of the Magi is the tender scene of the Annunciation and

Gaudí testing a number of steel tubes to reinforce and mark the axis of the columns in the Sagrada Familia.

General view of the Sagrada Familia:
an original sketch by Gaudí.
The architect must have first drawn it
in 1902 (replacing the original Greek
cross layout with a Latin cross);
he drew it again on various occasions
prior to his death in 1926.

the window behind it shows the symbol of the Paraclete, by whom the word was made flesh. In the upper loggia there is a grouping showing the coronation; its background – the rose window of the transept – shows the initials of the Holy Trinity, surrounded by angels intoning the Sanctus. The pinnacle of the great central lantern is formed by a cypress, symbolising incorruptibility and eternity, and landing on the tree are alabaster doves, the pure, predestined souls; it is crowned by a *tau*, the first letter of the name of God in Greek. Below is a figure of the Pelican, slashing its breast to feed its young and scattering drops of blood around the initials of Christ. Flanking the Pelican are two angels, holding an amphora of transubstantiated wine and a basket of eucharistic bread, the means of attaining incorruptibility. The backdrop is a vibrant array of flowering plants and a flock of birds on the wing, a reference to the nature of the Messiah, meant to stand out against the deep blue night sky of Christmas Eve.

To the right, on the inland side, is the door of Faith. In the centre of its pierced tympanum is Jesus as a child, speaking in the temple in Jerusalem, with Mary and Joseph looking on in amazement from below. In the lower portion of the archivolts are seen the Visitation and, on the other side, Jesus working in the carpentry shop. In the section above these archivolts is the Presentation of Christ in the Temple, showing the child being received by Simeon. In the terminal lantern are the highest mysteries of Faith: clusters of grapes and ears of wheat representing the Eucharist, the Hand and Watching Eye of Providence, the Immaculate Conception and the three-branched candelabrum, symbolising the Trinity. The flora and fauna used as adornment are Palestinian and in the colouring of the façade were meant to stand out on a background of ochres and siennas

To the left of the central door, on the seaward side, is the door of Hope. In the middle of its pierced tympanum is Saint Joseph, as Jesus' adoptive father, looked on from the archivolts by Saint Joachim and Saint Anne; below them is shown the Flight into Egypt and the Massacre of the Innocents. In the upper section is the betrothal of Mary and Joseph and in the lantern, Saint Joseph piloting the ship of the Church, guided by the Holy Spirit in the form of a dove perched on the sail. The pinnacle is the craggy form of Montserrat, a symbol of Hope, with the inscription "Deliver us". A background of mostly aquatic flora and fauna, including the Nile, was to be painted in different shades of green, to set it off.

Where the pinnacles of these doors begin, there is, in the centre, Jesus' initials above a cross, with the A and Ω, worshipped by two angels while two other angels collect the blood of the symbolic Pelican mentioned above. With the pinnacle of the door of Hope, there is a star with Mary's initials and with the pinnacle of the door of Faith, the initials of her chaste husband. These last two are lower down than Jesus' initials, which are accompanied by those of the Father and the Paraclete found on the pinnacles of Faith and Hope respectively. Thus, here on the façade, as well as inside the church and on the main façade, Gaudí masterfully showed Jesus' dual nature: his divine nature as a Person of the Holy Trinity, and his human nature as a member of the Holy Family.

On the lower bases of the three doors are the traditional Christmas birds, with turkeys in the centre, land birds to the right and water birds to the left, forming a picturesque pedestal for this monumental nativity scene. "Here, the people will find their elements, as the sage finds his in the signs of the Zodiac, placed in their positions in Bethlehem on Christmas Eve."

The Latin inscriptions *Iesus est natus, venite adoremus*, carried by two angels, and *Gloria in excelsis Deo et in terra Pax hominibus bonae voluntatis*, flank the Nativity. The name of Jesus, carved below the manger, is accompanied by the names of Joseph and Mary, on the central tambour of the columns dividing the doors.

The only façades finished are this one and the apsidal façade.

The Façade of the Passion is also called the Façade of Death or Sorrow, because it shows the principal events of Jesus' sacrifice. It therefore includes all of the sorrowful mysteries of the Rosary as well as the glorious mysteries of the Saviour's Resurrection and Ascension, completing Jesus' mission on earth.

In contrast to the Façade of the Nativity, with its smooth and attractive forms and abundant decoration, Gaudí planned the Façade of the Passion to be harsh and dolorous, leaving the walls desolate with a total absence of decorative elements, communicating to the spectator in this way the sense of consternation at the tragedy of Calvary. "We could not begin construction of the façades with this one, because it would not have attracted people. We began instead with the Nativity, because that it where it all begins, all of the hope and warmth.

The middle door, the door of Charity, has as the centre of its composition Christ crucified, with His Mother and the disciple whom he loved at his feet. This grouping occupies the column dividing the door. Flanking it are the other groups of onlookers at the Crucifixion; to the right, the good, silent onlookers: the holy women, Longinus and the good thief; and to the left, the bad, vociferating onlookers: the executioners, the Sanhedrin and the bad thief. "People who shout and insult are never right." Higher up, Jesus is shown instituting the new sacrament in word and deed, kneeling and washing his disciples' feet. Higher still is the Last Supper and the moment when the Eucharist was instituted. Lastly, in the tympanum, Christ praying in the garden of Gethsemane. Above this, in the middle of the crowning gallery, is a stairway leading to the empty grave, with the angel announcing the Resurrection to Mary Magdalene and the other two Maries. The image of the Resurrected Christ will appear in the middle of the window of the transept. Outside the portico and halfway up the two central bell towers of this façade, there will be a radiant Ascension, surrounded by the beating of wings of a myriad of angels.

As in the Façade of the Nativity, the side door on the inland side is dedicated to Faith. The lowest part shows the triumphal entry of the Messiah into Jerusalem, ridding on an ass, acclaimed as king by the people waving palm fronds and olive branches. Higher up, we see Jesus brought before the Jewish authorities: before Annas, whose servant is shown striking Christ, before Caiphas, who rends his clothing when the Redeemer affirms that he is the Son of God, and before Herod, who, irritated by Christ's refusal to answer, has him dressed in a fool's tunic.

The lowest part of the door of Hope, on the seaward side, shows a scene in terrible symmetry with the triumphal entry into Jerusalem: we see Jesus carrying the cross on the way to Calvary. Farther up Christ is led before the Roman authorities, and we see the flagellation, the crowning with thorns, the *Ecce homo* and Jesus condemned by Pilate, who washes his hands.

In contrast to the high lanterns and pinnacles that crown the portals of the Façade of the Nativity, here they are incorporated into a portico, supported on six columns and finishing at the top in a galleried pediment. This is a representation of Limbo, with the souls of the patriarchs, models of faith, on the inland side, and the souls of the prophets, who preached hope in the Messiah, on the seaward side. On the peak, carried aloft by angels, is the Cross, which Jesus, in his Charity, has converted from an instrument of shame into the sign of salvation. On the lower border are the biblical symbols of Jesus: the lamb of Abraham's sacrifice, offering itself humbly for immolation, and the lion of Judah, conquering death through resurrection.

The profound meaning of the façade is completed with the appropriate inscriptions. "Jesus said, *I am the resurrection and the life*. Therefore, over the entry into Jerusalem and the carrying of the cross, I placed the word *Via*, since we must follow the Lord, in both favourable and adverse circumstances; over the figure of Christ, naked and dead on the cross, will be the word *Veritas*, because the truth is naked, and among the scenes of the Mandatum and the institution of the Eucharist, will be the word *Vita*, since Love, the bread of heaven, gives us true life." In the archivolt will be carved the beautiful hymn of the Cross, *Vexilla*, sung in the Church on Good Friday. On the pediment will be the verse *Mors et vita*, from the Easter sequence, explaining the duel between life and death in the story of the resurrected Christ. The columns and arches of the portico show the crosses used by the different religious orders.

As in the Façade of the Nativity, an ingenious system of small stairways and passageways allows this iconography to be viewed from close up. In the Façade of the Passion, however, Gaudí added an inspired touch of his own. "All of the events of the Passion that took place indoors are set in niches and those that occurred out of doors are placed on projecting bases and can be seen from oriental-style galleries with grilles, such as may still be seen in the streets of Jerusalem."

Gaudí planned to place before this Façade of Sorrow a monument to Doctor Torras i Bages, the great renewer of our people's piety, who, shortly before his death, wrote his last sermon on the subject of sorrow.

The main façade is called the Façade of Life, because it depicts the teaching that was the purpose of the earthly life of the Divine Master and also because it presents a panorama of

Vignette produced between 1906 and 1911, from a drawing of the Sagrada Familia as a unit; an original by Gaudí.

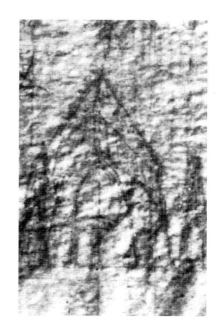

the spiritual and temporal efforts of human life and its meaning. The theological virtues are also present in this façade, in the Ark of the Covenant, the repository of God's Law, Noah's ark, the symbol of hope for mankind's salvation, and the house in Nazareth that was home to the love of the Holy Family. These elements are placed according to the arrangement mentioned above.

The composition is that of a grand portico with two rows of columns, at the back of which are seven doors, five of which lead to the naves of the church, with the remaining two giving access to the Baptism and Penitence chapels, which stand on either side of the portico, covered with vaults, lanterns and pinnacles. Above these emerge the four great bell towers and between the towers, white clouds carrying the tenets of the Creed, which are mankind's response to the Revelation and the teachings of Christ.

The Saviour's teachings are represented by the Lord's Prayer, the Beatitudes, the Sacraments, the forewarning of the Last Judgement, the revelation of the outer darkness into which sinners will expelled and of the glory to which those blessed by the Heavenly Father will be admitted.

The seven doors correspond to the seven sacraments, whose symbols they bear. Their lintels will be adorned with the entreaties of the Sunday prayers associated with the sacraments. The first on the left, which is the door to the Baptistery, has the symbol of baptism and corresponds to the entreaty, *Our Father in Heaven, hallowed be your name*. The next door, dedicated to extreme unction, with the words *Your kingdom come*; the next, corresponding to holy orders, has the words *Your will be done on earth as it is in Heaven*. The central door is dedicated to the Eucharist, the heart of spiritual life, with the entreaty *Give us today our daily bread*; next is the door dedicated to confirmation, with the words *and forgive us our sins, as we forgive those who sin against us*; then is the door corresponding to matrimony, with the inscription *and lead us not into temptation*; last is the door dedicated to penitence, with the final entreaty, *but deliver us from evil*. This door gives access to the Confession chapel, which will at the same time be the Chapel of the Holy Sacrament. It will house the tabernacle, as is fitting, and a Holy Thursday monument.

The Beatitudes are reproduced on the back vaults of the portico corresponding to the eight inner columns. Above their lintels is a frieze showing mankind bearing the burden of labour placed upon Adam and Eve, who are shown at the moment of original sin. Above them, Saint Joseph and the young Jesus in the carpentry shop give an example of manual labour. The other trades are also shown, those having to do with fire on the side of the Chapel of Penitence and the ones using water on the side of the Baptistery. The frieze is completed with allegorical references to the arts and sciences; below, on the columns flanking the door, are the acts of salvation, embodied in the fourteen charitable works.

The vitalising action of the Paraclete on mankind, completing man's experience of Christ's teaching, is represented on the seven outer columns of the portico. In the centre are the symbols representing the gifts of the Holy Spirit, at the base are the seven cardinal sins and at the top, their opposing virtues. The central column corresponds to wisdom, the virtue of charity and the sin of envy. To its left, intelligence, with the virtue of patience over the sin of wrath, fortitude, with diligence and sloth, piety, with generosity vanquishing greed. On the right are counsel, with temperance opposed to gluttony, science, with humility over pride, and lastly, the fear of God, with chastity opposing lust.

Final plan for the western façade, dedicated to the Passion, which Gaudí began to draw in 1911.

Along with the evangelising mission of the Son and the vitalising mission of the Holy Spirit, belongs the creative work of the Father. Thus, in the front vaults over these columns is a representation of the seven days of Creation, presided by figure of God the Father. The Trinity is completed by the Holy Spirit in the rose window of the central nave and the image of Jesus Christ crowning the highest lantern. In this image, Jesus is shown with the attributes of the Passion, which he will also wear at the Last Judgement.

Man's final destiny and implacable end also figure in this monumental composition. Death is represented by the tombs of the church's benefactors, under the floor of the church and in the crypt under the portico, the Last Judgement is present in the throne made ready for Jesus Christ, the Judge, Hell is shown on the vaults covering Calle Mallorca, with all of the manifestations of the Evil One, all of the idols of all mythologies and the instigators of all of the defections from the work of the Redeemer. Lastly, Glory is represented in the following manner: on the outside, above the portico and at the peak of each lantern, presided by the image of Jesus mentioned above, are the ranks of angels, among them "Saint John the Baptist and Saint Joseph, who are true angels"; and on the inside, between the frieze representing labour and the vaults showing the Creation, there is a second frieze, of the blessed, grouped in accordance with the Beatitudes and presided by the Virgin Mary, Queen of Heaven. Mary, with the figures of her husband and the young Jesus directly below, forming the Holy Family.

This is also, therefore, a condensed history of mankind: from the Creation, to the Fall, redemption by Christ, sanctification by the Holy Spirit and final destiny in eternal Glory.

On the platform leading to this façade, there are two elements of purification. In front of the Baptistery, a jet of water will rise twenty feet into the air and fall into four shells arranged around the Lamb of God, forming helicoidal cascades, evoking the four rivers flowing out of Eden and the fountains of the water of life in the Apocalypse. In front of the chapel of Penitence, there will be a tall, three-branched torch-holder, evoking the column of fire leading the chosen people in their pilgrimage. With the surrounding air and earth, this completes the medieval concept of the four elements of Creation.

At the corners of the cloister, corresponding to the four cardinal points, there are triple obelisks with the symbols of the cardinal virtues, the same ones that Gaudí placed in the lintel of the crypt of the church at the Colonia Güell. There are also elements referring to the ember days and their corresponding ordinations. From the middle of the back wing of the cloister emerges the cupola of the Chapel of the Assumption, in the shape of a mantle with its four corners held aloft by angels and topped by a crown. On the pediment are carved the first words of the Salve Regina.

Lastly, on the finials of the sacristy cupolas are the biblical prefigurations of Jesus: the grape-harvester trampling the vintage and the lamb offered for sacrifice, with verses of praise from the Apocalypse.

Interior. The renewal of the work of Redemption is carried out inside the church, through the re-enactment of the sacrifice, the administration of the sacraments and the teachings of the Church, and is represented in its three branches: the Church Militant, in the naves, the Church Penitent, in the crypt below the high altar, and the Church Triumphant, symbolised in a magnificent lantern of gilt metal and glass, an image of the Heavenly Jerusalem as described in the Apocalypse.

The help given to the Church Militant by the Holy Trinity is represented by God the Father, shown in a mosaic on the apsidal cupola, by the Holy Spirit, represented in the large, seven-branched lamp hanging below that cupola, and by the Son, on the crucifix of the high altar. Emerging from this crucifix is a grapevine, which climbs to form the baldachin and lamp, in keeping with traditional forms. This image of Jesus Christ also completes the representation of the Holy Family, with the image of Saint Joseph on the inside of the Façade of the Nativity and that of the Virgin Mary on the inside of the Façade of the Passion.

The teaching work of the Church consists of the instructive part of the Mass, the Gospels and Epistles, arranged according to the cycle of the liturgical year and recapitulating Jesus' life on earth. The Gospels are present in figured scenes on the railings of the gynaeceum and choir stalls, and the Epistles, corresponding to the Gospels, are present in inscriptions on scroll shapes in the capitals of columns. This didactic element is completed with the psalms and the main hymns of the canonical hours: the *Te Deum*, below the main dome, the *Miserere* in the side naves, the *Benedictum* of Zacharias, on the façade of the transept on the side of the Gospels, the *Nunc dimittis* of Simeon, on the opposite façade, and the *Magnificat* in the apse.

On columns of the transept and the adjacent columns, dedicated to the Evangelists and the Apostles, in relation to the exterior elements mentioned above, there will be texts referring to their commemoration and on the remaining columns, dedicated to the bishops, who continue the apostolic work, there will be texts referring to their feast days.

The vaults will show guardian angels descending and the Saints ascending.

The branching forms of the columns and their profusion will give people in the church the impression of "actually being in a forest; thus, around the base of the walls of the naves, there

The main, southern, façade of the Colonia Güell's church; an original by Gaudí; an old photograph of it is kept in the Ametller Institute of Spanish Art in Barcelona.

Mgr. Collell, Torres i Bages and Gaudí.

will be a depiction of winding streams, filled with fishes moving in the direction of the altar with their mouths open and other fishes moving away from the altar, with hosts in their mouths".

The apsidal chapels are dedicated to the joys and sorrows of Saint Joseph and "since we could not offer the place of honour to the Virgin Mary within the church, we dedicated the cloister, and the chapel placed there in the middle, to her". We mentioned above that the exterior of this chapel is in the traditional form of the platforms used in processions held on the feast of the Assumption. "The cupola is the mantle that compassionately covers the faithful; at the top is the Holy Trinity, ready to crown Mary, who rises to Heaven surrounded by ranks of angels. Halfway up, there is a gallery, with twelve angels holding the gifts of the Holy Spirit, symbolising the Virgin's crown. The base shows the death of the Virgin, the death of Saint Joseph, the presentation of Mary in the temple, accompanied by her parents, Joachim and Anne, and the wedding at Cana, where Jesus worked his first miracle, at Mary's request.

On the other side of the transept, leading to the cloister, there are four doors dedicated to the four manifestations of the Virgin most beloved by our people: Our Lady of the Rosary and Our Lady of Montserrat, on the Façade of the Nativity, in keeping with their joyful associations, and Our Lady of Mercy, redemptrix of captives, and Our Lady of Sorrow, on the Façade of the Passion.

Technical and Artistic Aspects

The constructive, static, optical and acoustic solutions arrived at by Gaudí constitute a work of technical perfection, in a unity of great plastic beauty.

The construction makes maximum use of the Catalan brick vault. This allowed the elimination of trusses and simplification of scaffolding. Gaudí later completed the divided vaults by reinforcing them and filling them with concrete, allowing their pre-fabrication and doing away with the need to proceed in complete sections, as in the medieval buildings. Another exceptionally wise constructive approach was to proceed by vertical elements, rather than in complete horizontal courses, since this is the only way to reduce the weight on the ground and prevent cracks when building an array of such substantial and varying heights.

As for the structure, Gaudí attained the ideal pursued by the architects of the great Gothic churches, that of eliminating the walls, making them completely into windows. He had the advantage over his predecessors of not needing buttresses and abutments and of having created a double roof of stone, one that is completely non-combustible, with the outer surface stronger than the inner one, a feat which, in the past, had never been accomplished. He achieved these extraordinary advances by inclining the columns and multiplying them in successive branches. "The real solution hinges on breaking up the inert masses and increasing the number of active elements, not few supports and large vaults, but many supports dividing the vaults into small sections. This is why there are so many keystones in the church and the thrust of the vaults is so low. The funiculus begins at the centre of gravity of the piece of the roof supported by each branch. This is the form of the tree – all of it a supporting structure – that, without any break in continuity, extends into the branches."

Gaudí liked to compare the stability and strength of the central naves of Cologne's Cathedral with the Sagrada Familia. Their spans are the same, in spite of the fact that the surface area covered by the latter is almost one quarter larger than the former; the section of the Sagrada Familia's columns is three times smaller and that of its abutments is four times smaller, and the latter are also partially hollow, to allow the passage of spiral staircases. The bell towers, which were square all the way to the top, finishing in a spire, in Villar's project, took on a stepped form in Gaudí's initial plans, like those of Santa María del Mar, and are octagonal for their top two thirds. He later made them circular, with a continuous parabolic curve, which, along with the fact that they are pierced, reduces their air resistance by more than one quarter in comparison with his original plan, and by almost half in comparison with Villar's plan.

Lighting is optimum. The lanterns of the lateral naves prevent the entry of direct light, only admitting oblique rays, which provide the best lighting for reliefs. When these rays are scattered upon striking the uneven surfaces of vaults and supports, they are diffused and give an intense light with no concentrated glare anywhere. Illumination is provided through translucent keystones in the vaults, consisting of alabaster globes, like stars. The space between these different-sized stars and the openings in the vaults is taken advantage of for providing an adjustable ventilation system.

Visibility of both the architectural ensembles and the decorative elements is excellent, inside and out. Upon entering the church through the main door, one sees the apsidal cupola at the focal point of the solemn progression of the vaults. The choir stalls are raked, allowing all of the singers a clear view of the altar, and foreshortened, not interfering with lines of sight to the windows immediately above and below them. The altar is raised one metre above the level of the presbytery floor and two metres above the floor of the naves, and is clearly visible from everywhere in the church.

On the outside, upon approaching the church, the masses of the domes grouped with the lower masses of the apse and the façades create a wide range of images of the building. The sizes of the statues, decorative elements, finials and carved inscriptions are in keeping with their different heights and are seen clearly from ground level.

As with the light, sound will not be concentrated, reverberated or echoed, owing to the diffusing surfaces of the vaults, columns and windows, and the priests' words and the choirs' songs will be heard clearly. Music will produce a surprising range of effects, owing to the different levels on which it is produced and the multiple choirs. On the outside, the acoustic characteristics of the bell towers were also studied carefully. They are equipped with inclined stone louvers to direct the sound of the bells downwards, so that it can be used to accompany processions as they move through the cloister or through the streets of the city. They can also be used to perform concerts of sacred music to solemnise the Church's major feasts. For this purpose, there will be three groups of a large numbers of bells, tuned to tones and semitones. Two of these groups will include tubular bells, played electronically from keyboards, some by percussion and some by compressed air. The other group will be made up of normal bells. After numerous experiments, Gaudí determined the shapes, lengths and thicknesses required to obtain the same intensity and purity of sound as from cylindrical tubes and normal bells, but using half the amount of metal.

The church's architectural composition is the development of a concept of tectonics based on the mountain of Montserrat, seen directly in space, incorporating architecture's greatest historical achievements, the structural experiments carried out with the chapel at the Colonia Güell, the plastic meditations of the Casa Milà and the polychromy of the Casa Batlló, shorn of any naturalistic excess and perfected through an intense process of revision over the architect's final twelve years that resulted in an ordering that is classical in its geometrisation.

The building has a pervasive unity, in spite of its numerous and varied bodies, which are placed in such a way as to constitute a system of repeated gradations that converge on the focal points from each viewpoint. The groupings of substantial architectural masses are all based on three principal volumes: the main façade and one lateral one, rising to the higher main dome; the portico of the Façade of Life, flanked by the lower and massive dome-shaped chapels; the apse and the dome of the Virgin emerging from the midst of the sacristies and the foreshortened bell towers of the transept crossing. In the same way, each façade consists of three fronts rising up to half of its height, like the bell towers and openings. Joining these elements is the grand base formed by the cloister and workshops, which, as a result of their smaller dimensions and placement in the foreground, underline the soaring height of the naves, which in turn produce a similar effect with the domes.

The measurements of all of these elements form a harmonic scale of simple proportions, based on a unit of five metres, with some exceptions, as required by external plasticity. This harmony of dimensions also extends to the representational figures, which are smaller on the Façade of the Nativity, larger on the Façade of the Passion and considerably enlarged on the main façade. This is not only meant to underline the symbolism, but also to be in proportion to the robustness of the architectural masses. Thus, the bell towers of the finished façade, with a circular section, have the smallest diameter, in harmony with the joined lanterns and the gentle forms and placid aspect of the grouping. The bell towers of the Façade of Life are also

Gaudí with President Enric Prat de la Riba and Dr. Reig (Bishop of Barcelona). November 30th, 1914.

circular and have the largest diameter, in proportion to their greater height and to the portico's robust lanterns, and they give a feeling of majestic serenity. The bell towers of the Façade of the Passion are elliptical in section, with a diameter midway between those of the circular towers, in keeping with the tortured forms of this façade and with the emphasis of edges, suggesting sharp pain. In the same way, the geometrical nakedness of the apse serves as a transition between the Façade of the Nativity and the Façade of the Passion.

The corporeality of all of these domed and conical masses is augmented by the intense concavity of the archivolts and especially of the porticoes. Representational sculpture and elements of flora and fauna always emerge from appropriately hollowed backgrounds. Polychrome details, more abundant and intense on these shaded, inset elements, complete the contrasting effect with the softer and less obtrusive colouring of projecting elements. On the larger walls, this colouring will be strictly the result of the patina, and colours will be applied to the finials and pinnacles, to accentuate them in reds and golds against the blue of the sky.

Inside, the modular canon also determines the dimensions of elements in relation to their situation and visibility. Instead of contrasts to accentuate the sculpted elements, here there is a harmonious range of light to illuminate – in gradations that intensify the sensation of space – the polychrome images of the vault and frieze mosaics. The dimensions of the representational and ornamental figures are also in keeping not only with the architectural elements, but also with their material, with opaque figures being larger and the translucent ones in the windows smaller, augmenting the apparent volume of the naves.

By day, then, the high white lights give the impression of forest clearings, and by night, under artificial lighting, they will take on the appearance of a shining constellation.

Gaudí's plasticity, based on the use of helicoidal and hyperbolic surfaces, combined appropriately by means of paraboloids, produces the surprising effect of a seeming elevation on the outside, and of luminous submersion on the inside.

INTERESTING UNREALISED PROJECTS

Among those of Gaudí's projects that were never carried out, some of which we have mentioned above, there are some that are particularly interesting because of their significance or magnitude.

Monument to the Virgin of Mercy. The Sanctuary of Our Lady of Mercy, in Reus, was built in gratitude for the end of a plague that had afflicted the city, thanks to the intervention of the Virgin. She had appeared to a young shepherdess who was guarding her flock in the place where the Sanctuary was later built, and told her that if the people of Reus were to go there in procession, she would end the plague, and this was done, with the promised result.

Gaudí's mother had inspired him with a tender devotion to the Our Lady of Mercy, which later culminated in the architect's desire to surround the Sanctuary with a monument that would perpetuate the moment of her apparition to the young girl, placing around it a flock of sheep and lambs lying down, which would have served as seats. Unfortunately, the town refused his offer, saying that they did not need any outside architect to re-work the project for the Sanctuary, since they already had one of their own.

Gaudí's preliminary project with his original idea has not survived; there is only one diagram, preserved at the Town Museum of Reus. We can easily imagine, however, that the man responsible for La Pedrera would have created a work of landscape art, and one of particular interest to visitors.

Royal emblems. On one of his visits to Montserrat, while working on the mystery to complete the monumental rosary described above, Gaudí, taking the poet's image one step further, conceived the idea of adorning the palace of the *Regina Cataloniae* with the royal crown and the barred shield.

"On the slender peak of the Cavall Bernat, I would have placed a large crown of wrought iron and glass, topped by a star and supporting a huge bell that would have made the peals of

Unfinished plans for a large hotel in New York; from the year 1908.

A model of the whole of the Sagrada Familia, to a scale of 1:25. The interior of the transept, published in El Pro on April 1st, 1918.

the *Angelus* resound over the countryside. The crown would have been reached by a stairway coiled around the spire of rock, which would also have served as an easily accessible vantage point for hikers. On the inner side of the crag, I would have placed Catalonia's shield, twenty metres tall, made of mosaic, which would have been visible from a distance of ten kilometres."

This work, aside from its artistic and symbolic significance, would certainly also have been one the worthiest and most valuable of Montserrat's attractions for visitors.

Plans for a Spanish Franciscan mission in Tangiers, Morocco (1892-1893) that was never built.

Monumental railway terminus. When the Madrid-Zaragoza and Madrid-Alicante railways decided to build their terminus in Barcelona, the company's distinguished president discussed the project with Gaudí. The architect, with his accustomed amplitude of vision recommended that they join their wide-gauge railway to the one serving the north in a monumental terminus. "I would have built the tracks in a loop, so that the trains could enter and leave the station without turning around, but this required a very large covered space without columns. As the thick iron supports are heavy and expensive, by making them work under pure tension, it would have been possible to construct an enormous canopy, with a distance of two hundred metres between supports. By varying their height and by using appropriate lighting, it would have produced an astonishing effect and the people of the countries with the world's great metallic constructions would have come here to marvel at it.

The Companies' technical experts and directors were taken aback at the project's magnitude and originality, in spite of the fact that it was based on the most economical solution. When they raised objections over the technical difficulties presented by canopies supported on funicular struts, Gaudí simply replied: "I will make the necessary preliminary tests and all of the problems will be resolved," but they were not convinced.

Renovations in Barcelona. When studies for the renovation of certain of Barcelona's monumental elements were commissioned to leading architects in 1907, some of those architects sought Gaudí's guidance on the subject and left the renovation of the Plaza Real and the buildings surrounding it in his hands.

Gaudí studied the many problems posed by this complex on the spot and began sketching his ideas for the project on blow-ups of photographs of the existing buildings. His approach was centred on making the work a homage to King Jaime: "It is not a question of setting up a statue of him on a pedestal, because, as his contemporary, King Louis IX of France was his superior in sanctity, our great king outdid him in political sense."

The architects also commissioned him to renovate the Salón de Ciento and the main stairway of Barcelona's Town Hall.

Unfortunately, and as is often the case with illustrious men, the immense possibilities offered by Gaudí's talent were not taken full advantage of, and these public works, which would have been a source of pride for our country, were not only never carried out, but they did not even reach the complete project stage. What is worse, almost all of the sketches and studies were lost during the Civil War.

THE WORK

CASA VICENS. Front and detail of the tower.

Preceding pages:
CASA VICENS.
Details of the railings at the entrance.

CASA VICENS.
Detail of the tower on C. Carolinas. This tower, supported by courses of thin brick, each projecting further than the previous one, caused such surprise that one of the bricklayers working on the job mentioned to Gaudí that he was worried that it would fall down straight away, to which the architect replied the following: "All you see are the projecting bricks, forgetting the reinforcement inside".

View of one side.

"The Arabs' courses of brickwork come closer to the *funicula* than the medieval Christian arches".

VILLA QUIJANO.
Eastern front.

"Architecture is the first plastic art: sculpture
and painting require it. Their worth depends
entirely on light. Architecture is about how
to order light; sculpture is a play of light;
painting is reproduction of light by colour,
which is light broken down".

VILLA QUIJANO.
Detail of a corner of the roof.

"Projecting and receding features must be
combined, with each convex feature i.e. in full light
- being matched by a concave one, in other words,
in the shade; the details of the lighted feature
must be well-defined, because they are visible,
while the feature in the shade does not require detail".

VILLA QUIJANO.
Columns by the entrance; western front.

A ventilation shaft opening in the form of a cubic stone masked by nine sunflowers on each side.

Watchtower.

"If a work of architecture is to be beautiful, each of its features must have its correct location, size, shape and colour. All of these qualities are intimately related in a work of architecture".

Will the moon
be intimidated
by the flowers' faces?
(Haiku by Matsuo Basho)

VILLA QUIJANO.
Detail of the ceramic sunflower.

"The flower is the image of the 'centre' and
as such is the archetypal image of the soul.
In alchemy, it symbolises the work (of the Sun)".

Preceding page:
VILLA QUIJANO.
Craftsmanship on the ground floor showing
clear Mozarabic influences.

Interior of the roof.

"Architecture is not stability. This is part of it,
but not the whole. An iron bridge is mechanical,
but not beautiful. Architecture is art; its frame
is mechanical, but lacks the flesh which will make
it harmonious, i.e. the form that envelops it;
once harmony has been achieved, it will be art".

CASA GÜELL.
Main entrance.

"Being lowish buildings, I decided to build them
of adobe brick, the most economical material,
and the one that conducts heat the least".

Detail of the pinnacle. By a strange coincidence,
the letter "G" is the initial of Mr. Eusebio Güell's
surname, as it is of Gaudí's.

The top of the pinnacle. Stone, brick with delicate
ceramic encrustations in the mortar, and artificial stone
together support this surprising antimony orange.

CASA GÜELL.
Main entrance.

"When a building has all that it requires using
the materials available, it has character or dignity,
which is the same thing".

CASA GÜELL..
Facade of the gate-lodge.
Dome and detail of the arabesque of the front.
Detail of the gate uprights.
Detail of the facade of the gate-lodge.

CASA GÜELL and dome of the gate-lodge.

Following pages:
CASA GÜELL.
Stables and coach house.

Coach house.

"The Greeks plastered and painted temples built of plain stone, and even painted the precious Pentelican marble, despite its quality and beauty".

Gate of forged and wrought iron.

Dragon. The Garden of the Hesperides (the daughters of Atlas and Hesperis) was heaped with celestial fruits, including the golden apples. It was guarded by a ferocious dragon, perhaps similar to the one depicted by this magnificent work of forged and wrought iron.

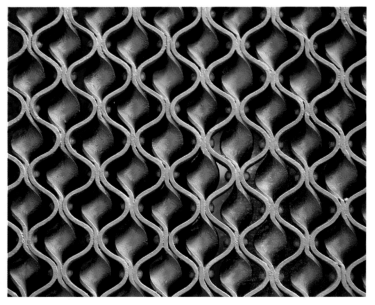

PALAU GÜELL.
Façade. Gaudí carried out eight studies for
the façade, which with their variations come
to twenty different drawings. The idea was that
it should be basically Gothic in style. While
the form is modern, the medieval spirit is evident
in its severe composition.

Detail of the railing on the door.

Detail of the arms of the façade. These cylindrical
arms of Catalonia topped by a mail helmet
and crowned by an eagle with spread wings are
a masterpiece of in iron which had to be personally
overseen by Gaudí owing to the difficulty involved
in producing it.

PALAU GÜELL.
Stables. Detail of the vault.

Column in the entrance hall-way.

"Güell is an aristocrat, because while one
who has money and shows it off is merely rich,
one who has money and does not flaunt it controls it,
he is in control and is therefore noble".

PALAU GÜELL.
Gallery to the rear.

"Nothing in the world has been invented.
The fortuity of an invention is that of seeing what
God has placed in front of everybody's eyes;
flies have been flying for thousands of years,
while men have not built airplanes until the present".

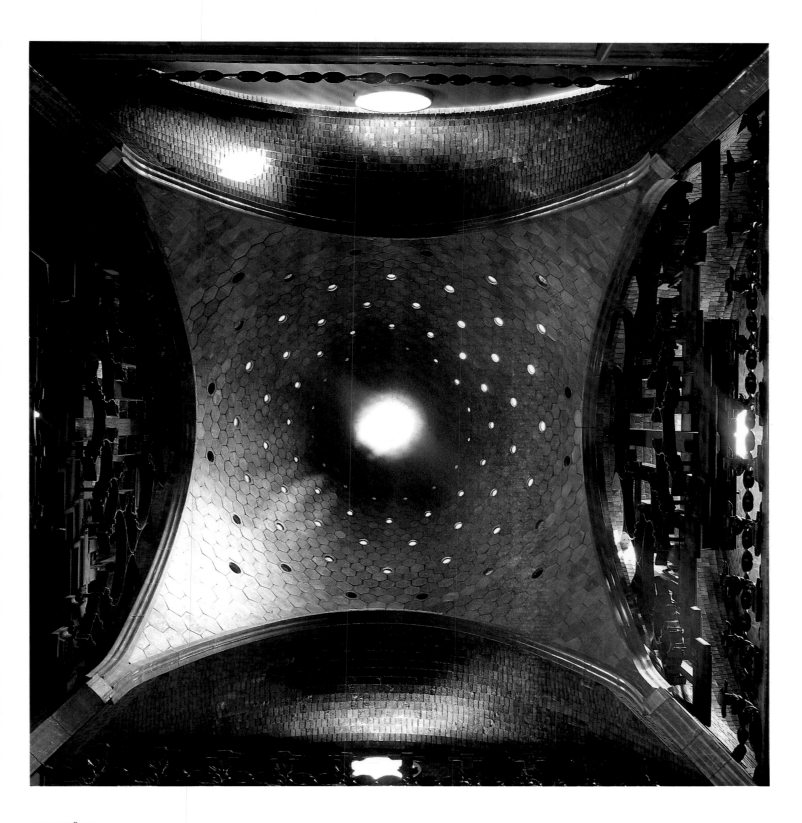

PALAU GÜELL.
Dome covering the hall.

"Man's intelligence is only able to work on one
plane, in two dimensions: it solves equations
with just one unknown. Angel's intelligence
is in three dimensional, it goes directly to work
in space. Man cannot act until he has seen
a thing carried out; to begin with,
he just follows trajectories, lines on a plane".

Preceding page:
PALAU GÜELL.
Dining-room window.

"All thought whose form does not fit in with the spirit of the times is ignored. Thought must fit the form, and all rhetoric must be avoided".

Inside the gallery.
"In order to do something well, to begin with, you must love it, but you also require technique".

Detail of the gallery's exterior ceramic work.

"Repetition is the only productive method: Verdaguer always repeated, copied and corrected his poetry".

PALAU GÜELL.
Detail of a hyperboloid capital.

Base of a column in the living-room.

"Elegance is related to poverty; but be careful
not to mistake poverty for misery".

Detail of the columns on the first floor.

"Material and measure are one and the same thing,
as a soft material demands few, large elements,
while a hard material requires many small elements".

PALAU GÜELL.
Conical roof of the Hall. An opening to let light in.
Weather-vane with the symbol of the city.
Conical roof of the hall. Openings in the lower part,
gas-lit in the original plans.
Detail of a radiant brass sun.

PALAU GÜELL.
Chimney. The truncated pyramidal form covered
in ceramic shard reminds one of the cones used
in weaving in Güell's factory.

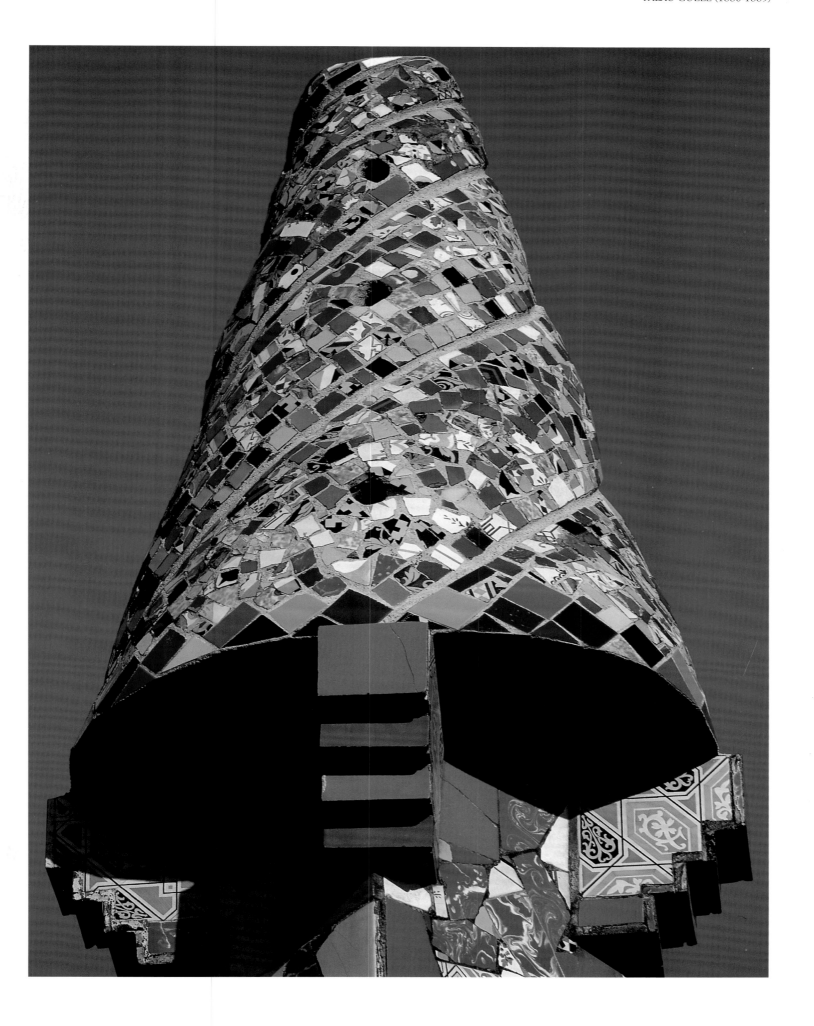

SAINT TERESA OF JESUS SCHOOL.
Detail of the façade. Note the simplicity
of the construction methods used,
and the many imaginative designs.

Following pages:
SAINT TERESA OF JESUS SCHOOL.
Corner pinnacle. The projecting brick buttresses
support the pillars at the end of the façade,
while the religious community's arms are in a recess
between them, in front of a helical column.

Entrance to the porch.

The main corridor on the ground floor.

Preceding pages:
SAINT TERESA OF JESUS SCHOOL.
First-floor corridor.
Vestibule and corridor on the first floor.
The religious community's arms in front of a helical column.

Parabolic arches of a ground-floor corridor.

Ceramic anagram on the main front.

EPISCOPAL PALACE IN ASTORGA.

"Whenever I had to design a building in some traditional style,
I attempted to place myself within the circumstances and
characteristics of that style. Then, and only then, could I create
with complete freedom".

Entrance porch.

"Continuous forms are the perfect ones. Usually, a distinction
is created between supporting and supported elements,
which is obviously wrong; there are those which both support
and are supported. This distinction creates a degree of imperfection".

EPISCOPAL PALACE IN ASTORGA.
Capital in the central Hall. Natural and Mudéjar
forms are in harmony in this capital whose top
is finished with stalactites.

"The capital provides a solution by unifying
the various elements: if there are not several elements
to unite, it is not a capital".

Chapel. Base and capital together.

EPISCOPAL PALACE IN ASTORGA.
Ceiling of the Bishop's chamber. The extremely
long arches contrast with the shortness
of the slender columns that support them.

Throne room. Detail of the fine work
of the baldachin.

Following pages:
Arches in the meeting room. The versatility
and fine combination of the forms evoke heavenly
palaces.

Apse of the chapel.

EPISCOPAL PALACE IN ASTORGA.
Throne room. Stained-glass windows. The slender arches
supporting the windows (decorated with the bishops'
coats of arms) remind us of nearby León cathedral.

Following pages:
EPISCOPAL PALACE IN ASTORGA.
Main entrance hall.

Interior of the conclave room.

Preceding pages:
CASA DE LOS BOTINES.
Façade.

Detail of the façade. It fits in harmoniously
with the Los Guzmanes palace,
despite the different style used by Gaudí.

Detail of the façade. Lobulate arch of the main
doorway, and free-standing sculpture,
by Matamala, of St. George killing the dragon.

BODEGAS GÜELL.
Northern front.

BODEGAS GÜELL.
Details of the northern front.

Preceding pages:
CASA CALVET.
Façade.

Detail of the bay window. Gaudí's liking for the Baroque style is obvious
in the continuous ornamental sculpture of the domed canopy supported
by the pillars of this bay window.

Façade.

CASA CALVET.
Door-knocker on the front door. A masterpiece in iron,
where the most fantastic baroque design made great demands
on the smith's abilities. When the knocker hits the door,
a cross with four equal arms beats the knob which stands
out from a background of four shining ridges.
Detail of the railing of a trilobate balcony.
The house-number.
Detail of the railings on the front door.

CASA CALVET.
Balcony.

Detail of the façade.

"I made the archaic Doric column in Güell Park,
just as the Greeks would have produced it in a
Mediterranean colony; the Bellesguard mansion is Gothic
and modern in equal measure, while the house in C. Casp
is closely related to the Catalan Baroque. It is all a question
of immersing oneself in the period, the ambient,
the means and capturing their spirit".

BELLESGUARD MANSION.
Façade. Although he had already abandoned
the Gothic style, Gaudí returned to it in his maturity,
in this work in homage to King Martin the Humane.

Detail of the ceramic bench of the façade. A shark
enveloped in the "M" of Maria, and the four bars,
symbol of Catalan hegemony in the Mediterranean.

Façade. Round-arched doorway, similar to those built
in King Martin's days, cut from white granite,
while the local slate has been specially chosen
in dark grey, green, brown and yellow tones.

BELLESGUARD MANSION.
Details of the main front.

Following pages:
BELLESGUARD MANSION.
Spire topped by a ceramic four-armed cross.

"The aim of art is to achieve the effect aimed at in its totality".

Courtyard with staircase.

The Magi stained-glass window.

Preceding page:
BELLESGUARD MANSION.
Loft. Brick structure supporting the roof.

Loft. Details of the structure.

Preceding pages:
PALMA DE MALLORCA CATHEDRAL.
Main apse.

Detail of the main apse.

PALMA DE MALLORCA CATHEDRAL.
Decoration of the main altar.

Rose window. Lighting by Gaudí.

"This is not a renovation, but a restoration,
not however in the restricted meaning of remaking
features in a specific style or period, sacrificing those
from other ages, but in the sense of returning things
to their place and their true function. To be precise,
it is an architectural-liturgical restoration".

GÜELL PARK.
Stairway leading to the marketplace.

"The architect is a man who combines. He is capable
of seeing things as a whole before they exist;
he places elements and coordinates them in relation
to one another at just the right distance.
This intuition is where the work's static quality
and its polychrome feel are to be found".

Chimney tower of the southern gate-lodge.

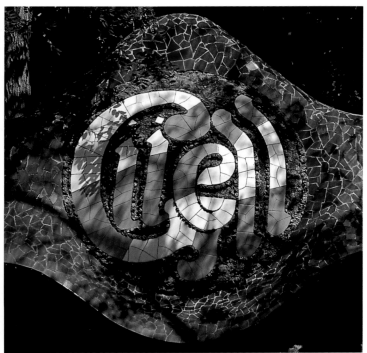

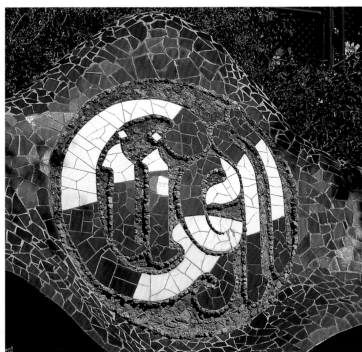

Preceding page:
GÜELL PARK.
Enclosing wall.

"Decoration has been, is and will continue to be colourist
in nature. None of nature's realms fall into the monotony
of the nuance; this is why we use polychrome for some
or all of our architectural features.
The sun is the Mediterranean land's great painter!"

Ceramic covering of the wall. Details of the various
polychrome ceramic symbols including the name of the site.

Following pages:
GÜELL PARK.
Outer front of the northern gate-lodge.

"Virtue is found in the middle; Mediterranean means the middle of the earth.
Here, light at forty-five degrees is what best defines objects and shows their shape.
This is where the great artistic cultures have flourished, owing to the quantity of light,
neither too much nor too little. The Mediterranean provides a concrete view of things,
where genuine art must be rooted. Our artistic strength is the balance between
sentiment and logic".

Scalloped roof of the northern gate-lodge. Detail of the ceramic fingers
rising to a depiction of *Amanita muscaria*.

GÜELL PARK.
Details of the windows of the southern gate lodge.

Inner front of the southern gate lodge.

"All styles are organisms related to nature; some produce an isolating rock,
as the Greeks and Romans did; others make mountains and peaks, like the Hindus.
All agree on minimal support (which is where character lies), that is to say the column
and the horizontal supported elements; the whole forms a tree; and its proportions
are similar to those of the human body, which means that it is not a genuine tree
(as a building has a different function from a wood), but a tree-man. This allows
us to understand and explain all styles: the Egyptian, Greek, Byzantine,
Gothic tree-man and so forth".

Preceding pages:
GÜELL PARK.
Detail of the central stairway. The salamander proffers
water from the mother rock.

The serpent of knowledge issues from the symbol
of the Catalan people.

GÜELL PARK.
Detail of the salamander.

GÜELL PARK.
Detail of the serpent.

"The feelings are never wrong, because they are life
(if they could be wrong, that would be death); it is the
head which is no more than the control panel, just a
part, that makes mistakes. As a result, a people cannot
be killed. Voices can be stifled, valves can be closed,
but then the pressure increases, and the danger of an
explosion grows. And if too many valves are blocked,
the explosion becomes inevitable".

GÜELL PARK.
Entrance stairway. Ceramic shard wall.
Gaudí reserved polychrome for places which were
less open to the rigours of the weather and better
protected against the rain. He also used coloured
stone or polychrome glass to cover walls built
with everyday materials.

"Patience is strength, which is why those
without patience are powerless".

GÜELL PARK.

Samples of ceramic shard work from various parts of the park.

As a young student in the school of architecture, when shown Greek
art, it did not appear strange to him, but rather quite familiar;
he felt it to be somehow natural.

"Everything to do with mosaic is Greek, it comes from Constantinople".

GÜELL PARK.
Hall of columns of the Doric order. The bottoms
of the columns are clad in white ceramic shards,
which counters their excessive slenderness
for an archaic Doric style. The capitals' abacus seem
squashed by the weight above. The drops hanging
from the fluting or triglyphs of the frieze are realistic
in form, rather than geometrically stylised.

"I have come to retrieve architecture where
the Byzantine style left off".

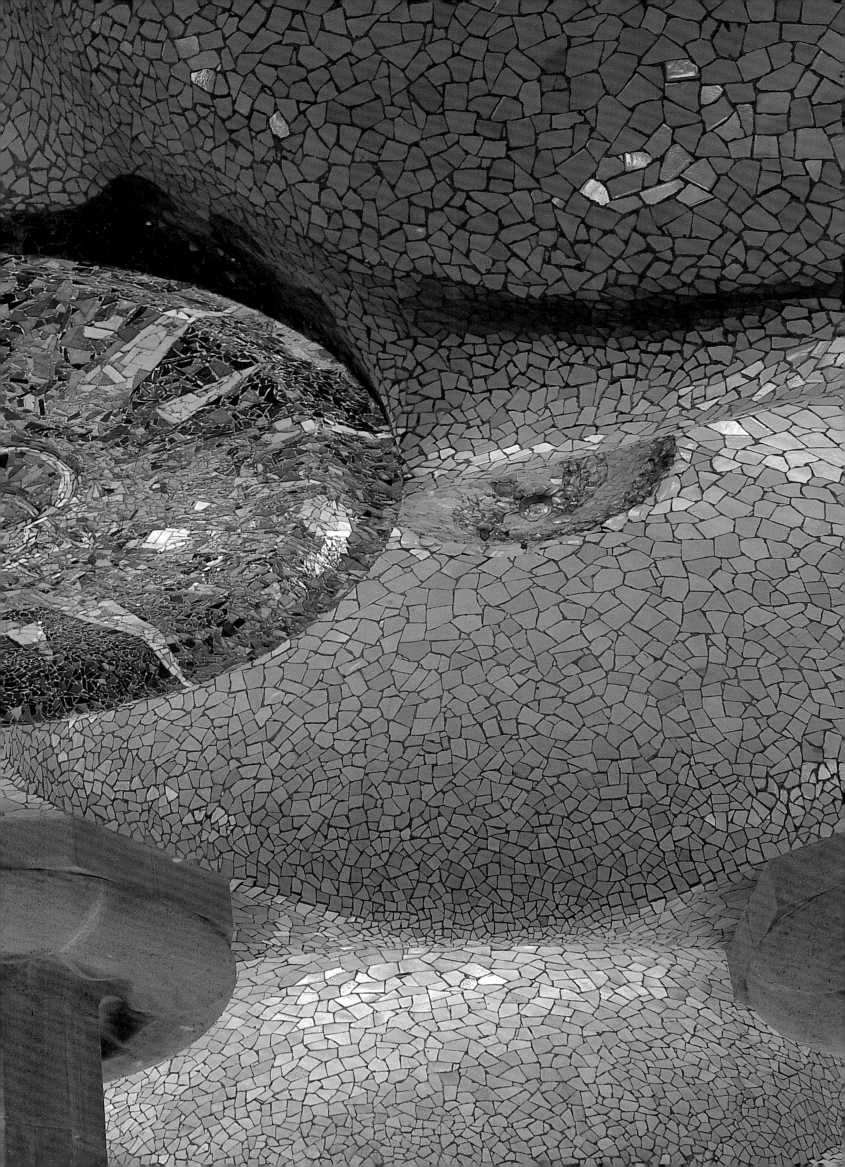

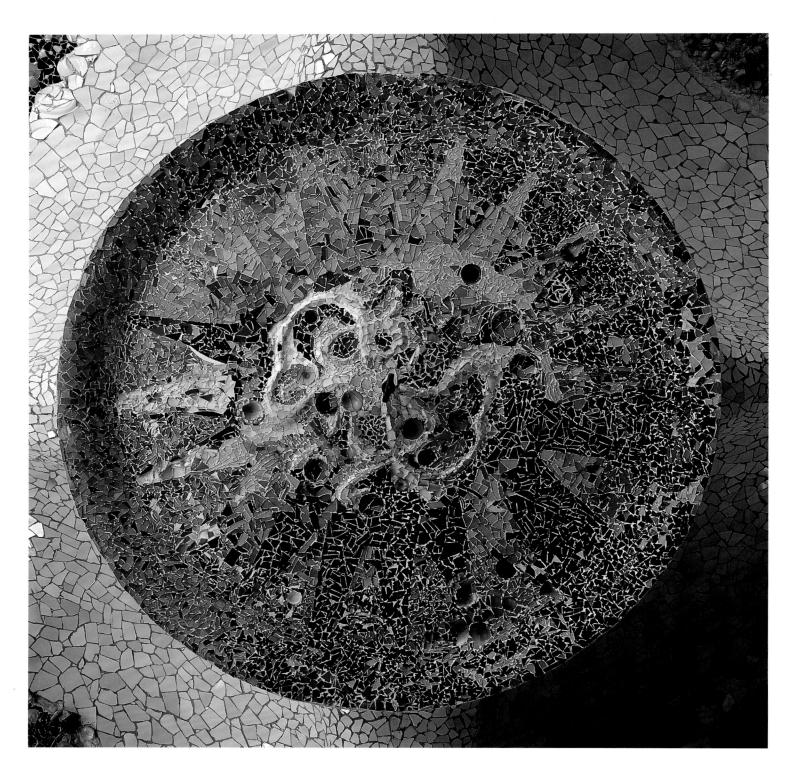

Preceding pages:
GÜELL PARK.
Inside the Doric hall of columns. The ceiling, made
of domes supported by slightly curved beams,
and the white ceramic shard decoration give one
the sensation of floating on a gravity-free
Mediterranean held in place by the columns.

Ceiling of the hall of columns.

"Love of truth must come before all other loves".

GÜELL PARK.
Ceiling roses done in coloured glass.

"Sagacity is superior to science. The word comes from
sapere, which means to savour (wisdom); it refers
to the fact. Wisdom is wealth, it is a treasure; science
provides us with certainty about what we examine; it is
required to keep counterfeit coins out of the treasure".

GÜELL PARK.
Roof of the hall of columns, topped off
by the ceramic bench-parapet.

"I am a geometer, which means a man
of synthesis. Only the Mediterranean peoples have
understood geometry, and to find it we must go
back to the Greeks. Geometry of surfaces does not
complicate construction - rather it simplifies it".

GÜELL PARK.
Ceramic bench-parapet.

"Their artistic value apart, these monuments are
a major asset for the country that they are located in.
An asset that provides a visible return: the money
left by the tourists who go there to visit them.
Important business centres also have a flourishing
artistic life".

GÜELL PARK.
Detail of the ceramic bench-parapet.

"There are no teachers in the arts: the only teacher
is oneself. What exist are means: societies and
organisations that provide models and information
on artworks, directly or through reproductions.
But there are two dangers involved here: Schools of arts
and crafts contain and will continue to contain
charlatans who talk but produce nothing; texts
and reproductions can be found in magazines,
and many are satisfied with that. Schools,
art circles and magazines are secondary".

GÜELL PARK.
Detail of the ceramic bench-parapet.

"Harmony is the essential quality of any work of art;
these works are the product of light, which provides
relief and decorates. I suspect that the Latin word *decor*
either means light or something closely related
to it expressing clarity".

Preceding pages:
GÜELL PARK.
Detail of the shard mosaic of the bench-parapet.

"One cannot move ahead without a basis in the past, taking advantage of the efforts and advances of the generations that have gone before us. We must know the past if we wish to be capable of producing something worthwhile, of avoiding the errors of the past".

Detail of the shard mosaic of the entrance staircase.

"Painting uses colour while sculpture uses shape to express existing organisms: figures, trees, fruit... using exteriorities to put across the interior. Architecture creates an organism and so it should be ruled by laws which are in agreement with nature: architects who do not submit to this rule produce muddles rather than artworks".

GÜELL PARK.
Detail of the arcade bearing the raised pathway.

"Harmony, or what is the same thing, balance, needs contrast, light and shade, continuity and discontinuity, concavity and convexity, etc".

Sculpture from the arcade bearing the raised pathway. The only human figure that we find in our stroll. The position of the arms is particularly meaningful, as are the basket piled with stone held on its head, and the female figure's totemic androgenous face.

GÜELL PARK.
Arcade bearing the raised pathway. Detail of a column.

GÜELL PARK.
Arcade bearing the raised pathway.

"Beauty is truth's lustre, and the lustre seduces every one;
that is why art has that universality. Science, on the other hand, reason,
is for the prepared intellect".

GÜELL PARK.

Detail of the parapet with benches and flowerpots.

Parapet with benches and flowerpots.

Retaining wall.

Curve in the arcade bearing the raised pathway.

"All works of art must seduce (this is what makes them universal in nature, as they attract everybody, the learned and the layman alike); if a bid at originality eliminates this seductive quality, it is no longer a work of art".

Preceding pages:
GÜELL PARK.
Arcade bearing the raised pathway.

"Beauty is the lustre of Truth; as art is Beauty, there is no art without Truth.
In order to find Truth, one must be very familiar with the beasts of creation".

Entrance stairway. Detail of the mother rock.

Entrance stairway. Detail of the grotto spring.

"There is no freedom in heaven; as it is in possession of the whole truth,
it is subject to it. Freedom is a temporary, passing thing".

COLONIA GÜELL.
The crypt and arcade-cum-ramp of the planned church.

"In building this church, I intended following a tradition of ours,
the Mediterranean tradition. All architectural styles have come into being around
the temple, and all innovative art must do so too. True art has always come
from the Mediterranean: Syria, Egypt, Greece, Italy etc."

Under the arcade.

"Creation continues, with the Creator making use of his beings:
those who look for the laws of nature in creating new works cooperate with the
creator. Imitators do not cooperate. Originality involves returning to the origin".

COLONIA GÜELL.
Window on the eastern front.

Under the arcade.

"Life is a battle: one needs energy to fight, and that energy is virtue. This can be
maintained only by cultivating the spirit, in other words, through the practice of religion".

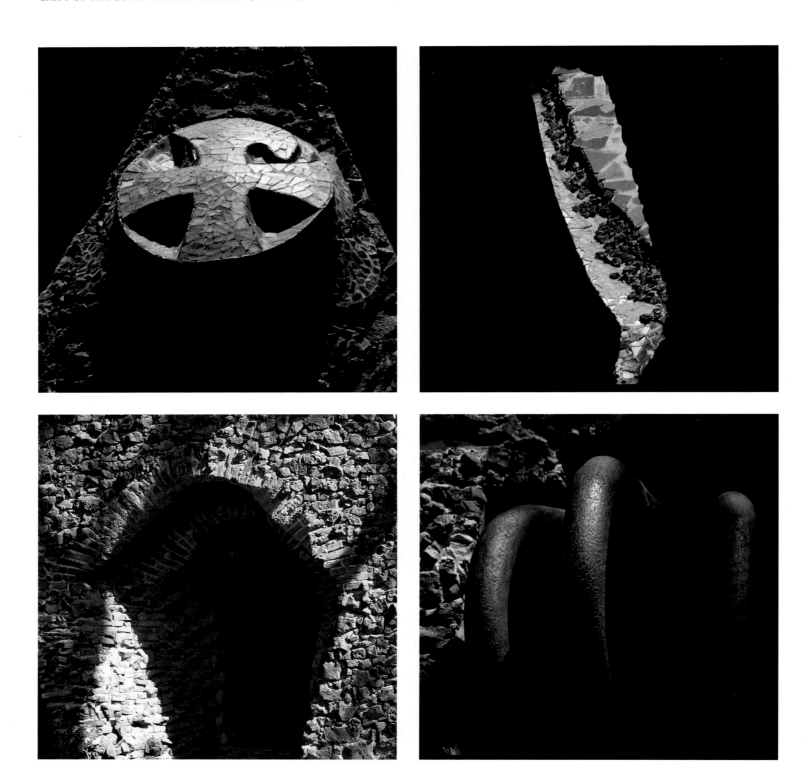

COLONIA GÜELL.
Bacular cross in a circle.
Parabolic gutter over one of the windows on the western wall.
Opening on the southern wall.
Railing on the southern wall.

"Thought is not free, but the slave of Truth. Freedom
does not spring from thought but from volition".

COLONIA GÜELL.
The pointed surrounds of the eastern windows.

"It is good to blame yourself even if you are blameless, because it makes
the truth shine without seeming to; it is an excellent thing to do because
the worst enemy of work well done is a good opinion of yourself,
and this is why you should persist in dominating and minimising it,
although at first you will not manage to do so".

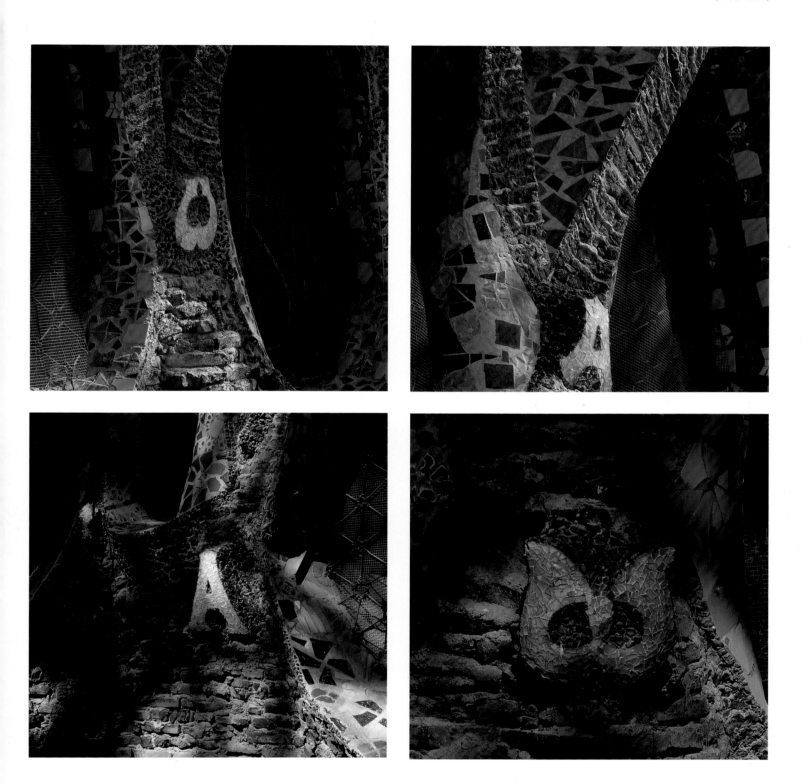

Preceding pages:
COLONIA GÜELL.
Window on the western side. The railings were made from spikes
recycled from Güell's textile mills.

Details of the eastern wall. The symbols of alpha and omega
adorn the exterior of the crypt's eastern wall.

"It is worthwhile observing the use that the liturgy makes of light,
which is the basis of all decoration, as the various colours spring from it
when broken down. Light prevails in all of the plastic arts. Painting does
no more than copy it, while architecture and sculpture provide it with motifs
where it can play with an infinite number of nuances and variations".

COLONIA GÜELL.
Under the arcade. Long bench.

"Building workers build walls by dropping two plumb
lines and running a horizontal line between them;
when a line falls out of plumb (which happens more
frequently than one might think), the wall that
the bricklayer believes he is building flat turns into
a paraboloid. We decided to use this shape from the
very beginning, and on seeing its beauty and
the possibilities it offered, we adopted it for the walls
and the arches".

Following pages:
COLONIA GÜELL.
Under the arcade. A view of the magnificent basalt palm-tree
that supports the arches here used by Gaudí for the first time ever
in the history of architecture.

Detail of the basalt pillar in the centre of the arcade.

Space under the arcade.

COLONIA GÜELL.
Entering the arcade.

Arcade ceiling. The first of thirteen ceramic
Santa Eulalia crosses, of varying colours
(green, brown, black and blue) which indicate
the symbolic itinerary through the portico.

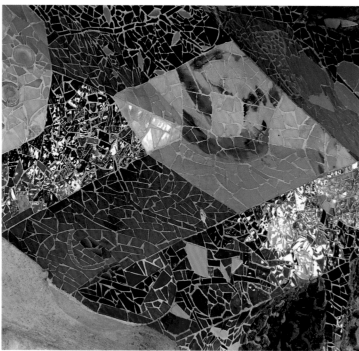

COLONIA GÜELL.
Ceramic compositions:
Detail of the pink cross.
Detail of the IHS.
Detail of the cardinal virtue of fortitude.
Detail of the cardinal virtue of prudence.

Following pages:
COLONIA GÜELL.
Arcade ceiling. The last of the crosses on the route through the arcade.

Lintel and ceiling of the arcade. Rhomboidal ceramic composition
above the lintel of the doorway into the crypt, and the black cross of Santa Eulalia.

COLONIA GÜELL.
Interior of the crypt. Detail of the benches
designed by Gaudí with specially inclined backs
to encourage the faithful to concentrate
on the liturgy.

Following pages:
COLONIA GÜELL.
Holy water font. An extraordinary work in wrought iron
holding up the huge shell used as a holy water font.

Interior of the crypt.

"Man is the instrument of a higher being, man only
enjoys freedom within the bounds of the triangle".

COLONIA GÜELL.
Interior of the crypt. Detail of the ceiling,
using hyperbolic paraboloids built of brick.

Interior of the crypt. Two of the four magnificent
basalt plinths, columns and capitals rough-hewn
with blows of the stonemason's hammer.

CASA BATLLÓ.
Façade and roof.

Detail of the façade.

"Work grows out of cooperation, and this can only
be based on love; that is why those who have
the seed of hatred within them must be set apart".

CASA BATLLÓ.
Detail of the roof. Gilt inscription of the Holy Family.

CASA BATLLÓ.
Balcony. The plaster model for these balconies'
parapet was found in the Church of the
Holy Family's model workshop.

Following pages:
CASA BATLLÓ.
Detail of the roof.

"Iridescence is caused by the material exfoliating;
the surface of mother of pearl has these fine reliefs,
which is why it produces iridescence;
glass scratched by quartz dust become iridescent
in the long run, which also happens
with Arabic ceramics".

CASA BATLLÓ.
Details of the first-floor balcony.

CASA BATLLÓ.
Detail of the wavy decoration of the façade.

CASA MILÀ.
A view of the whole building.

"The work is intended as a monument to Our Lady of the Rose, as there is no such
monument in Barcelona. And as it will be extraordinarily expensive,
I have decided to skimp on the building: the casa Milà is built on the cheap,
using materials with a high coefficient of resistance".

Detail from a corner of the façade.

"I would not be surprised if this house were to be converted into a hotel
at some time in the future, owing to the ease with which its rooms can be
rearranged, and the large number of bathrooms".

CASA MILÀ.
Front facing C. Provença. Detail of the balconies.

"The stone's patina, enhanced by climbing plants
and flowers on the balconies will provide the house
with a constantly-varying colour scheme".

CASA MILÀ.
Front facing C. Provença. Detail of the balconies.

From which flowering tree
I cannot say
but what a perfume!
(Haiku by Matsuo Basho).

Following pages:
CASA MILÀ.
Detail of the front facing Passeig de Gràcia.

CASA MILÀ.
Front facing C. Provença. Details of the stonework.

"Proportion, which is the law relating the parts with the whole and the features with each other can and must be specified exactly. Studying nature can give us a degree of intuition, but studying technical advances and materials gives each street and each building its particular character; supports made of cut stone have and always have had a relationship between base and height, and when art has flourished, the upper and lower limits have never been exceeded. The Greeks fixed their limits with the Parthenon and the Erechtheum, while the cathedrals fixed them during the Middle Ages. Considerable gains can be made in the correlation between parts by simplifying the elements used in construction".

CASA MILÀ.

Passeig de Gràcia front. Details of the stonework.

"Simply-expressed forms have greater grandeur".

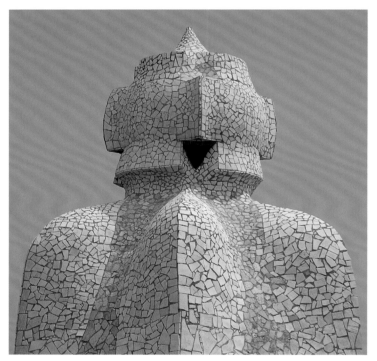

CASA MILÀ.
Details of the stair exits. The stairs that lead from the attic to the roof are covered
with these symbolic shapes, which were originally intended as part of the entourage
of a huge statue of Our Lady of the Rose in the company of the angels.

Stair exit. Detail of the broken stone mosaic. Detail of the spiral:
this could symbolise universal evolution, or spiritual development.

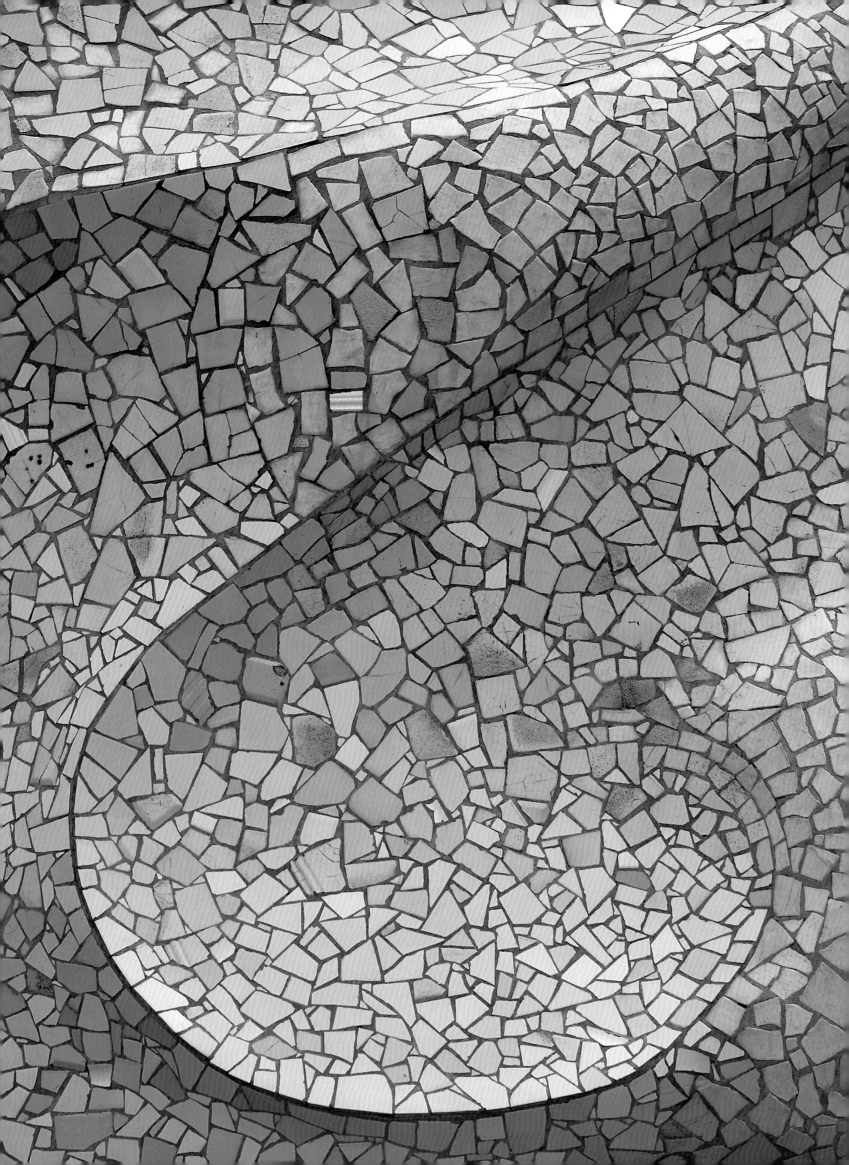

CASA MILÀ.
Detail of the chimney.

Following pages:
CASA MILÀ.
Detail of the stair exit and chimney.

Detail of a group of chimneys.

"Producing any object involves ensuring that it is ruled
by the laws of creation (without which, lacking consistency,
it could not continue to exist); and to do so, experience is a requisite,
as this is creation's seal of approval".

CASA MILÀ.
Detail of a ventilation shaft.

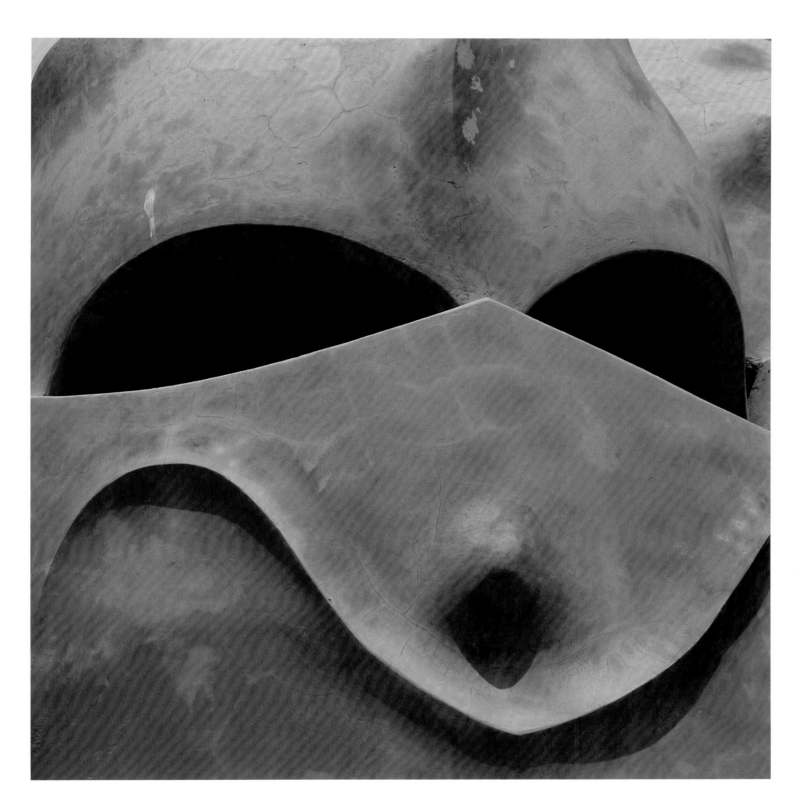

CASA MILÀ.
Detail of a chimney.

"Archetypes are numinous structural elements of the psyche
which have a degree of autonomy and energy of their own,
which allows them to attract whatever contents of the consciousness
that suit them. These are not hereditary depictions, but rather certain
innate predispositions to form parallel representations,
which I called the collective unconscious".
(Karl Jung)

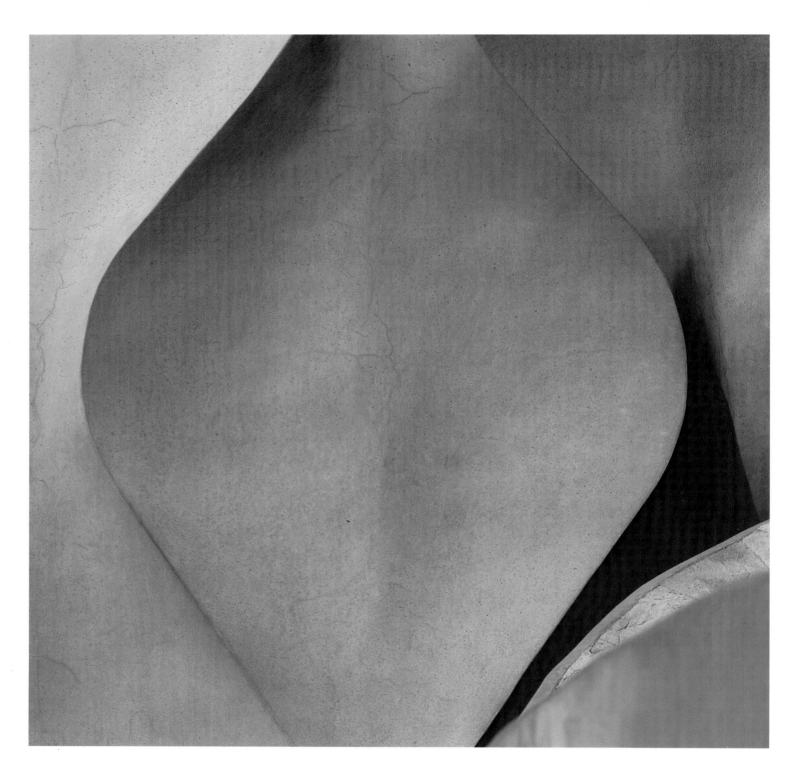

CASA MILÀ.
Detail of a stair exit.

"In symbolism, the particular represents the general,
not as dream nor as shadow, but as the live,
immediate revelation of the inscrutable".
(Goethe)

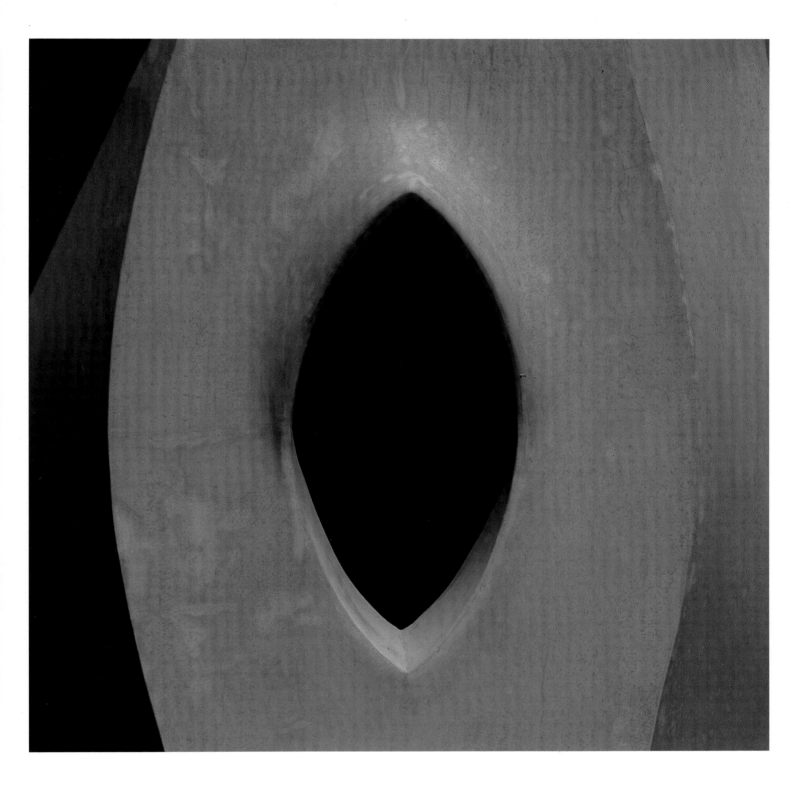

CASA MILÀ.
Detail of a ventilation shaft.

"The symbol is the ideological manifestation of the mystical rhythm of creation, and the degree of truth attributed to the symbol is an expression of the respect that man is able to give to this mystical rhythm".
(Marius Schneider)

Following pages:
CASA MILÀ.
Courtyard. Detail of the windows.

"My original intention was to build a double ramp around the larger courtyard, in order to be able to reach the apartments by car. This would have needed a broad ramp, and so a great deal of space (twice that of the building), and therefore large entrance halls and very high apartments".

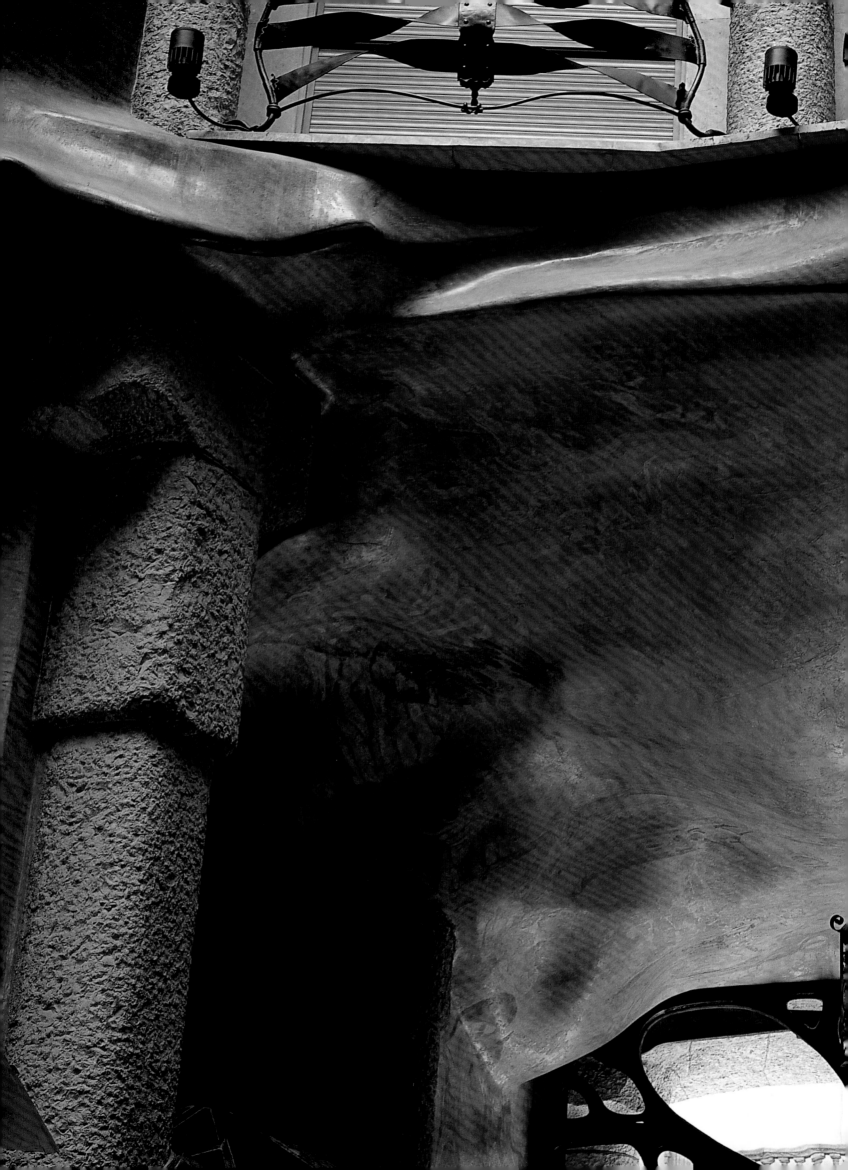

Preceding pages:
CASA MILÀ.
Entrance from C. Provença. Detail of the ceiling.

casa Milà. Detail of the courtyard.

CASA MILÀ.
Detail of the courtyard.

"Now that studying vegetation and botany has become widespread,
certain plants have great decorative possibilities, which adapt and attach themselves
to geometrical combinations with great ease, just as the same plants do in the wild.
When a full depiction of a plant is not sufficient, a complement can be used,
but one that has a rather rigid conventionality which will make the lifeless plant
form seem genuinely leafy, fresh and lush".

Following pages:
CASA MILÀ.
Interior column on the first floor.

Detail of an interior column on the first floor.

"The great book, always open but which requires an effort to read,
is the book of Nature; all other books are taken from this one, and what is more,
they include man's mistakes and interpretations. Two revelations exist: on the one
hand, the doctrine of Morals and Religion, and on the other, that which is guided
by events - the great book of Nature".

Preceding pages:
CASA MILÀ.
Detail of plasterwork from the first floor.

Attic. Detail of the structure.

"Elegance is close to poverty;
but be careful not to mistake poverty for misery".

CASA MILÀ.
Attic. Detail of the structure.

"All things are worthy of attention, they are all very complex; and behind it all,
we always find mysterious corners where we our limitations cause us to get lost.
A brief glance at the facts is a bestiality (a consolation for the beasts).
In order to penetrate things, you have to go patiently after them; patience
is constancy in the inevitable difficulties".

CASA MILÀ.
Mechanical study for the arcade, crypt, chapel and domes
of the Colonia Güell church.

"I calculate everything: first I suspend a number of weights to find the *funicula*;
then I shape the resulting *funicula* with forms and materials; then I revise
their weights, sometimes changing them slightly again. In this way, I find the logical
shape resulting from the requirements. I found the *funiculas* for the Church
of the Holy Family in a graphical manner, and those of the Colonia Güell
by experiment. But the two procedures are the same, one is the fruit of the other.
This procedure of trial and error is required by the limited human intelligence.
The basis of all reason is the rule of three, mathematical proportion, syllogism".

CASA MILÀ.
Attic. Details of the structure.

"Paraboloids, hyperboloids and helicoids cause the incidence of light to vary constantly; they have a wealth of nuances of their own which does away with the need for decoration and modelling".

SAGRADA FAMILIA.
Nativity front.

"In the Holy Family church, all is providential; its location in the centre of the city, and in the centre of the plain of Barcelona; the church is the same distance from the hills as it is from the sea, from Sants and from Sant Andreu, and also equidistant from the Besòs and Llobregat rivers".

Following pages:
SAGRADA FAMILIA.
Detail of the Nativity front.

"This front expresses life's hope and joy; the bell-towers finished by episcopal motifs and the veneration 'Hosanna-Excelsis' are dedicated to the apostles whose statues can be seen below (St. Barnabas, St. Simon, St. Judas and St. Matthew)."

SAGRADA FAMILIA.
Detail of the Nativity front. The palm-tree, symbol of heaven on earth,
supports the two angels of the apocalypse.

Detail of the Nativity front. As in Gothic cathedrals, monstrous animals
can be seen in the lower parts.

SAGRADA FAMILIA.
Nativity front. Detail.

"The Church is continually growing, and this is why it is headed by a bridge-builder
(Pontiff); churches are bridges leading to Glory. I also admire the exquisite tact
with which the Church accepts all styles, and receives the homage of all the arts.
The Church makes use of all the arts, those occupying space (architecture, painting,
sculpture, goldwork...) and those occupying time (poetry, song, music...).
The liturgy provides us with lessons in the refined aestheticism".

SAGRADA FAMILIA.
Nativity front. Detail of an angel playing the harp.

"In heaven, we will all be choir members."

SAGRADA FAMILIA.
Nativity front. Detail of the birds. All bird species existing in Catalonia can be seen
in this part of the façade. Birds symbolise superior states of existence. The soul-bird
ascending, and also the messenger dove, which descends carrying heavenly powers.

"The sagrada familia is the product of the populace,
and so displays their way of being. This work is in the hands of God and the volition
of the population. The architect, living among the people and turning to God,
does his work. It is Providence, in its highest designs, who carries the work forward".

Preceding pages:
SAGRADA FAMILIA.
Nativity front. Detail of the grottos of the Faith, Hope and Charity doorways.

"The church's decoration is based upon saints ascending to Heaven from the Earth,
and angels descending from Heaven to Earth".

Nativity front. Detail of the produce of the earth.

"Everybody will find something in the church, farmers see cocks and hens,
scientists see the signs of the Zodiac, theologians the genealogy of Jesus,
but the explanation, the reason behind it all, only the erudite will know it,
and it must not be divulged".

SAGRADA FAMILIA.
Nativity front. Detail of the signs of the zodiac depicted.

SAGRADA-FAMILIA.
Nativity front. Detail of the spire from the entrance of Our Lady of the Rose.

"The superior has to make the most important sacrifices, the subordinates
can carry out small ones that do not require his presence. The superior must give
them the means required to carry out his orders and to make good their lacks.
Pity the man who complains about having bad assistants".

SAGRADA FAMILIA.
Nativity front. Detail of the balcony crowning the image of St. Judas.

"Artists are carried away by their vanity because they are creators
of a piece of Glory; but what they ought to do is attempt to produce
true Glory and satisfy their spirit therein without boasting of having done so".

SAGRADA FAMILIA.
Detail of the Nativity front. St. Joseph steers the ship of the church
with the assistance of the Paraclete in the shape of a dove.

"This church will be finished by St. Joseph".

Detail of the Nativity front. Depiction of Montserrat.

SAGRADA FAMILIA.
Nativity front. Detail of a bird ascending to the highest.

"A man without religion is a man without spirit, a mutilated man".

SAGRADA FAMILIA.
Detail of the Nativity front. The monumental IHS consists of the cross with the alpha
and the omega as background for the name of Jesus, with two adoring angels,
and two more collecting the blood spilled all around. Above is the white pelican,
symbol of the sacrifice of the Eucharist, feeding its offspring with its own blood,
accompanied by two angels carrying the sacramental bread and wine.

Preceding pages:
SAGRADA FAMILIA.
Detail of the Nativity front. The cypress tree, symbol of eternity, flanked by two stairs of seven steps. In it are a number of white alabaster doves representing purified, predestined souls.

Nativity front. Detail of the cypress stairs.

"The 'Sanctus, Sanctus, Sanctus…' in helical arrangement are dedicated in threes to the Father, the Son and the Holy Spirit. That dedicated to the Father will be gilt, as the colour that best represents light; that dedicated to the Holy Spirit will be orange, and that dedicated to the Son will be red, which is the colour used in the liturgy to symbolise martyrdom. The Holy Spirit is in the centre because it communicates between the Father and the Son, which is why its colour lies between the other two".

Following pages:
SAGRADA FAMILIA.
Nativity front. Details of the bell-towers.

"The shape of the towers, vertical and parabolic, is the union between gravity and light. A great luminous light will be placed at the very top of the church, like natural light which also comes from the sky. On nights of solemn religious occasions, this light will provide the church with life and sumptuousness, as well as being the city's best decorative feature."